GOAL SETTING FOR WRITERS

A Step-By-Step Roadmap to Success

HOLLY LYNE

Goal Setting for Writers: A Step-By-Step Roadmap to Success

Published by Weaver of Words Press
UK

Copyright © 2020 Holly Lyne

H.B. Lyne asserts the moral right under the Copyright, Designs and Patents Act 1988 to be identified as the author of this work.

Book Cover design by Olivia Pro Design
Interior Formatting by Evenstar Books Ltd.

ISBN 978-1-913673-08-6 (paperback)
ISBN 978-1-913673-09-3 (ebook)

hblyne.com

Contents

Intro   *1*

Chapter 1: Where Are You Now?   *7*

Chapter 2: What's Your Characters Motivation?   *26*

Chapter 3: Get SMART   *34*

Chapter 4: The Hero's Journey AKA Make a Plan   *47*

Chapter 5: The Nitty Gritty of Your Task List   *62*

Chapter 6: How To Actually Achieve Your Goals!   *73*

Chapter 7: Hold Yourself Accountable   *92*

Chapter 8: Overcoming the Central Conflict   *98*

Chapter 9: Embrace Your Spark of Madness   *120*

Conclusion: The Hero Returns   *124*

Resources   *127*

Get Your Free Planning Guide   *129*

Please Leave a Review   *130*

Acknowledgements   *131*

About the Author   *132*

Fiction by H.B. Lyne   *133*

Intro

If you've picked up this book, it's a fairly safe bet that you are looking for some help setting and achieving your goals.

Maybe you're a champion at setting goals, but when it comes to meeting them it all falls apart.

I've been setting and studying goals for twenty years. I've tried all the tricks and learned what does and doesn't work for me. Everything that I've included in this book has been extremely effective for me and other writers that I know. I've been part of accountability and mastermind groups and have seen the tremendous achievements of those I've worked with over the years.

I've written this book whilst running my own business as a fiction author, home educating my kids, running a second author business with my business partner, maintaining a home and social life, and generally keeping all the damn plates spinning!

I've been able to smash my goals, but not the plates, by using the systems I'm going to share with you in this book.

I have every reason to believe that they will work for you too.

As with all things, however, you ultimately have to find what works for *you*. I will share what I've learned, and you can choose what to implement and what to adapt, depending on your individual circumstances and needs. Not all of my tips and tricks will be applicable to you, and that's fine. We're all on our own paths. But if this book can help you get closer to accomplishing the things you want out of your author life, then I'll consider my job well done.

There are a lot of people out there dishing out advice on setting goals and getting things done. You'll find people who claim to have a single, unifying system that is foolproof and guaranteed to work. They've cracked it and figured out what you MUST do in order to succeed. That's quite a masculine approach and, in my opinion, not really fit for purpose in the twenty first century.

I'm not going to tell you to get up before dawn, or to speak a certain way, or to change the strategies that you've already honed and that work for you. You have strengths of your own, and they will work well for you if you double down on them. I'm not going to place demands upon you, or tell you how hard to work (and it always seems to be "harder than now", doesn't it?). In fact, I'd go as far as to suggest that there is virtue in doing less. *What?! But isn't this about getting more done?!* No. It's about getting done what truly matters. You do not have to do all the things in order to be successful.

"PROGRESS ISN'T MADE BY EARLY RISERS. IT'S MADE BY LAZY MEN TRYING TO FIND EASIER WAYS TO DO SOMETHING."

—Robert Heinlein

There are many paths to success. What is success anyway? Your idea of success won't be the same as mine and that's fine. That's good and healthy. We all have our own unique dreams, desires, and plans. How we get there is equally unique to us.

The systems in this book are not guarantees and they aren't universal. They're adaptable. The only really guaranteed route to success is to chart your own course and get there in your own way. That, at least, sets you up for a much better chance of success.

In this book, you will learn how to identify where you want to go and I'll share some powerful tools and planning methods to help you get there.

Why this book might not be for you

If you're sensitive to coarse language, bad jokes, and generally don't like the whole idea of making plans, then this probably isn't the right book for you. If you're seeking guarantees with no expectation of you needing to make any effort to make changes, then this also isn't going to work. I'm providing tools, but it's up to you to implement them.

We've all read non-fiction books before that are packed with useful tips and then quickly forgotten everything because we didn't take the time to actually work those tips into our daily lives. I want this to be different for you. I want this book to revolutionise your goal setting so that you can say goodbye to un-met goals and soar into a future where you are constantly checking off your task list with a grin and feel that swooping sense of pride and accomplishment when you do exactly what you set out to do!

Where I've set exercises for you, please take the time to do them. It will work best if you do them as we go along, but I do understand if you want to read the whole book first and then work through the exercises at once.

The Roadmap

So that you can embark on this journey prepared for what lies ahead, here is a quick summary of the plan.

We're going to start by figuring out your starting point. Where are you now? We can't very well work out where we want to go or how to get there, if we don't know where we're starting from. This might be a bit of a bleak beginning, depending on your circumstances. It's worth making the effort, however, in order to make the most of our journey together. Chapter 1 will deal with the mistakes you may have made in the past that have brought you to this book. It can be hard confronting these things, but the benefits of doing so are well worth it.

We get to the exciting task of planning for the future once we know where we're starting from. Please don't skip ahead. Put in the hard work for maximum results. I'll share with you some stress-busting tips to help you to get into the right zone for implementing the planning that we're going to do. Let's calm your life down a notch to create space for progress.

Chapter 2 gets into the big, juicy and optimistic shit. We'll figure out your Big Why so that we have a destination for our road trip.

In Chapter 3, we'll cover the nuts and bolts of my goal setting system. I'll share the most effective method that

I've found for actually accomplishing goals. We'll also figure out what kind of writer you are. Spoiler alert: you'll need to know that in order to set the most effective goals.

Throughout Chapters 4 and 5, we're going to tackle the really nerdy bits that I love! The planning, organising and refining of details. Don't roll your eyes, this is my gift to you. You're welcome.

By the time we get to Chapter 6 we'll be speeding along Route 66 with no traffic in sight, the top down, and the pedal to the metal! I'll show you how to kick ass and finally do all of the things you've decided you want to do. No more abandoned projects, forgotten goals and depressing task lists with nothing ticked off! Say hello to success!

Every good story needs a conflict, so in Chapter 8, we'll look at the obstacles in the road and deal with them consciously and effectively so that our road trip doesn't get too far off track.

Finally, we'll round off our journey together by reminding ourselves what it's really all about.

So, are you ready to refine your ability to set and accomplish goals? Pack your notebook, water bottle, and a change of underwear. We're going on a road trip and this is your guidebook. Now, get in the car, I'm driving.

Chapter 1: Where Are You Now?

Why bother to set goals?

As a writer, you'll be familiar with the concept of plotting. It's one of the questions you'll face most often: are you a plotter or a pantser — someone who begins writing without a pre-planned plot? That and "where do you get your ideas?"

This binary choice is one of the big, persistent myths in the industry. It's actually a whole spectrum, and many of us move around within it from one project to the next. And for the record, "pantser" is *not* the preferred term for many of us. I use the term "discovery writer", but I also like the phrase, "write into the dark".

Regardless of where you fall within that spectrum, you'll know that having a road map for where your story is going can be a useful tool. Don't get me wrong, I'm actually a discovery writer myself. I often begin a new book with just a premise, with no bloody idea where it's going to go. I've made my way through periods of my life like that too. It works for some people remarkably well.

But I've learned that having a plan for life actually helps me out, both day to day and over the longer term. The only reason that I can be confident that my books have good flow and structure when I've written them into the dark is because of many years of practice and over three and a half decades of absorbing stories in all mediums. Even so, I often need to pause part way through a story to sit down and think about where I want it to end up.

If I was planning a road trip I'd have a destination in mind and I'd look at a map to plan my route and ensure I don't get lost. There's still plenty of opportunity for improvisation along the way. Where we'd stop, who we'd meet, and what adventures we might get into. All of that fun can still be had with a plan.

Without a plan, is it really even a road trip? How far would you get? Would you get to the end of the day and realise you didn't pack any clean underwear, don't have enough money for a hotel, and end up going straight home?

Setting long- and short-term goals can help to ensure that you don't drift through your days not accomplishing much of anything. It might be enough to decide you're going to write a book. Maybe you'll actually do it with no further planning than that. In a 2002 survey, 81% of Americans said they wanted to write a book. Most of them never have or will. What makes you any different?

The difference is that you're reading this book. That tells me that you're interested in setting and achieving your goals.

The second part is the most important one. Anyone can set a goal. "I'm going to write a book." There, done, easy. Actually doing it is another thing altogether. There's a reason most New Year's Resolutions are forgotten by February. Saying you want to do something gets you nowhere if you don't have a plan for getting there.

In this book I'm going to walk you through my goal setting process and share what has worked for me and countless other people. I'll give you a system that you can use to set the right goals and actually achieve them when you say you will.

Is there ever a wrong time to set goals?

There are times in life when setting goals is the last thing you should do. Some events require a unique mode: crisis mode.

I don't use the term lightly. I'm talking about certain major events: bereavement, a job loss, a pandemic.

There are times when all that matters is getting to the end of each day. If you don't know where your next meal is coming from, or whether you'll still have a roof over your head in the morning, then it's not the time to worry about your word count.

When there are forces outside of your control having a serious impact on your day to day life, then give yourself time and don't try to make plans beyond what you can reasonably manage. That's absolutely fine. If a loved one recently passed away then you have every right to shelve every plan and idea for as long as you need to. Just in case you need it: you have permission to put your goals aside. You do not owe anyone that book, blog post, or podcast episode. When it feels like there's a heavy weight pressing on your chest, you deserve the chance to stop to catch your breath. Hold your space and shut out the stuff that doesn't matter right now.

When does Crisis Mode end?

Whenever you feel ready.

There is no definitive answer that will be right for every person in every situation. But what I can tell you is that you'll recognise the moment when it comes. If your situation has meant that you haven't been showering or getting dressed most days, then the day you get up and feel like you want to do those things (and maybe even eat something other than dry toast) is the start of things getting better enough to set a small goal. And I do mean small. Try "today I'll go for a walk", or "today I'll write a sentence of my novel".

You'll have that moment. Whatever your crisis is. Because all things pass, despite how it can feel when you're in the thick of it.

My experience with crisis mode

Three years ago I was in a serious collision. My husband and I were driving along a country road, having just dropped off our children at my parents' house. It was a route we knew well and had never encountered problems on before. I had my laptop open in my lap in the passenger seat and was working through suggestions from my editor on my fourth novel, while my other half drove. Suddenly, we swerved left and my eyes were wrenched up from my screen. I stared in horror as we were struck down the driver's side of the car by a van and we were sent flying off the road straight towards a drystone wall. We ploughed right through the wall and into the field beyond. Our airbags were deployed, but I have no memory of that happening. In fact, after striking the wall there is a gap in my memory.

I must have blacked out for a few seconds because what I experienced was the sound of screaming from very far away but coming closer. It was a shrill scream that went on and on in an almost continuous tone. Eventually I became aware that it was *me* screaming. We were at a stand-still in the field, our airbags limp and the air filled with dust. I could not stop screaming.

My door was wrenched open and my husband was there, I hadn't been aware of him getting out of his side of the car. It was only when I was eased out of the car, shaking from head to foot, that I realised that my computer wasn't in my lap. The first vaguely coherent words from my mouth when I stopped screaming were a desperate cry of "my laptop!" It lay smashed to pieces in the footwell of the car. My wrists were in excruciating pain.

When the airbag went off, my laptop, which I was holding in both hands, had been forced towards me, snapping back both of my thumbs, before sliding off my lap. My right wrist required a splint and I couldn't type or write by hand for months. I had to have physiotherapy and even so, both of my wrists have never been the same since.

Needless to say, that whole incident created some significant obstacles! I was weeks away from the launch of my book. By some great act of willpower, I managed to get the book out on time. I had it backed up, so had only lost the edits that I had already gone through. But I didn't publish anything new for almost two years. I didn't write at all for months. NaNoWriMo got me going again, but I didn't finish that project and have pretty much abandoned it. For most of the following year I couldn't write anything either. My wrists had recovered, but my mental health hadn't. The timing of the crash couldn't have been worse. That fourth book was the conclusion to a series that meant a huge amount to me. Once it was finished I began to question whether I would ever have another idea again.

The crash put me in crisis mode. Albeit a delayed one. Obstinacy and adrenaline pushed me through the launch but then the event caught up with me and I was forced to a halt. But after a while, I drifted out of crisis mode and into survival mode. There was no longer a temporary, but extreme set of circumstances pressing on me. It had become a prolonged period of struggle.

When there is no crisis, but you're stuck anyway

In the normal course of things it's perfectly common to set goals and not make any progress towards them.

As you're reading this book, I'm going to hazard a guess that this is you much of the time. You're interested in setting goals, you set them all the time. But nothing ever comes of them. Am I right? There are a few reasons why this might be the case. Let's take a look at some of them and go over some potential solutions one by one.

Survival Mode

In addition to crisis mode, there is another crippler: survival mode.

Some events in life are just plain challenging. There is no "crisis", but there's an ongoing issue that keeps you from moving forward. I'm talking about chronic mental and physical health conditions, poverty, being a carer for a loved one with additional needs, and other difficult, long-term problems.

When you're in survival mode you might only be capable of accomplishing small goals, like cooking a healthy meal for the first time in weeks, or applying for two jobs today. If you're under a huge amount of stress, writing can be the last thing on your mind.

Cortisol is a hormone that floods our brains when we're under stress. It's supposed to help us when we're in "fight or flight" mode, but when we're under constant stress the adrenal glands can keep making cortisol even when there is no imminent threat to life or limb. Having too much of this hormone in our systems can lead to serious health problems such as:

- Trouble sleeping
- Reduced concentration
- Memory loss
- Digestive problems
- Weight gain
- Depression and anxiety
- Headaches
- Heart disease

So it's no wonder you aren't making progress on your book, or advancing your ambition to earn enough from writing to be able to quit that stressful day job!

Reduce Stress For Effective Goal Setting

Anything you can do to take control and lower your stress levels will help you get back to a place where you can set effective goals for your writing. If there is nothing you can actively do to get out of the situation that is causing you stress, the key will be reducing the effect of the situation on your stress levels. (I am in no way qualified to advise on stress management specifically, so I urge you to seek appropriate support for your situation if need be.)

I have personal experience of living in survival mode, and I know how insurmountable it can feel. Throughout this book I'm going to be sharing tools that I've found helpful. I experience high levels of stress almost daily. I've figured out a range of things to help me to manage my goals and writing in spite of this challenge. You might find them useful too.

If you're in survival mode then there are simple goal-setting techniques you can use to ease your way out of it, and we'll get to that in a later chapter. But for right now, take action to reduce the stress that you're under. Your health comes before your writing or career goals.

Yoga

Studies have found that regular yoga practice lowers the level of cortisol in the blood. Yoga and other forms of stretching and gentle exercise can clear your mind and relax your muscles, and can be a great way to get you back both physically and mentally into a space where you are able to focus on writing.

Scheduling Relaxation Time

If you don't plan it, it's less likely to happen. Let this become your mantra! Work and family commitments can consume every waking minute if you let them. You need to schedule breaks in which to do other activities. Whatever relaxes you, organise it, plan it, enjoy it! Days out with friends, date nights with your partner, even just some time lounging in front of the TV, *schedule it*.

This might sound incredibly rigid, if you want to be able

to set and achieve effective goals it's essential to take beneficial breaks and turn off your work brain.

Get Out In Nature

Nature is vital to our physical and mental health. Walking in natural surroundings for just 20 minutes a day has been found to have a profound effect on cortisol levels.

Calming nature sounds lowers blood pressure as well as cortisol. So nature has been proven to help people worry less and to feel more content. Getting out for a short walk, or even just play some soothing natural sounds, can be a simple way to help you get back into a space where your writing goals can begin to feel achievable.

Exercise

More vigorous exercise is incredibly helpful at lowering cortisol levels. High Intensity Interval Training (HIIT), strength training, cardio, whatever appeals most to you personally, just pick something that you can do regularly. It might be rock climbing or skiing, or maybe skipping down the street with your kids. There are lots of ways to work exercise into your life, whatever your situation, and any extra movement you can manage will only have a positive effect on your ability to focus more on your writing goals.

Tickle Fights and Dance Offs

Seriously. Laughter is one of the best ways to reduce stress. Taking time out to do something that makes you laugh, whatever that may be, can be hugely beneficial to your overall mental health, and get you back in the right head space to pick up your pen or fire up your laptop!

Emotional Freedom Technique (Tapping)

EFT is an excellent resource for reducing stress. It's far too big a topic to go into great detail here, so if it interests you I recommend you search YouTube for videos that explain and demonstrate it. The basic principle is that you tap on key acupressure points on your face and upper body while thinking about a problem and talking through it. You relax your body and mind and then use affirmations to form more positive neural connections in the brain in order to change the way you think and feel about a situation. Each time you think a thought it strengthens that neural pathway, like a well-trodden path through a forest.

As a bare minimum, tapping acts as a pattern interrupter, halting repetitive negative thoughts and giving you a moment to re-frame a situation. If you think this might be something beneficial to you in terms of getting your focus back to writing, I highly recommend giving EFT a try.

Avoid the Mainstream Media

I admit this is an entirely personal tactic. For me, the constant barrage of negativity in the news has been a cause of stress my entire teen and adult life, and I've had extended periods of completely ignoring the news. That's been made harder with the dominance of social media in our lives; it's hard to ignore the headlines when you have friends who constantly share them. But I've learned to be selective in what sources I listen to, and I rarely seek out news from mainstream websites or channels. Whether or not you trust these sources, the sensationalism and the emphasis on one crisis after another can be extremely detrimental to your mental health.

If you find the world news overwhelming, consider restricting your consumption of it. This may in turn give you more time and space to work on setting effective goals for your writing projects.

Turn Off Your Phone

Horror! Unthinkable! Is being constantly contactable a source of stress in your life? How about the temptation to respond to every notification?

I have long been a vocal advocate of turning off notifications in order to minimise distractions. I turned mine off in 2016 and have never looked back. For Facebook pages and email, you can set up an autoresponder to reply to anyone who contacts you and respond personally later.

I could write a whole book on this topic. Suffice it to say, notifications are not only a distraction, they can be bloody stressful in themselves! Other people's agendas and demands can leave us with a constant hum of interference that causes a low level of persistent stress. So if you recognise that feeling, turn off notifications, (do that anyway) and consider turning your phone off completely for extended periods of the day. It will help with the previous point of avoiding bad news too. If your phone is off, it's that bit harder to just quickly check social media for any news updates that might upset you. And you'll find you can invest the time and stress that you save yourself straight back into your writing goals.

Writing

Many of us find writing to be the ultimate stress-reliever. But it can also be a source of stress in itself. There's a growing trend to dismiss writer's block as a myth. Something to be believed in or not, rather than an objectively genuine phenomenon. The dictionary definition of writer's block is:

"The condition of being unable to think of what to write or how to proceed with writing."

It is perfectly obvious that this is experienced by many writers around the world and throughout history.

Saying you don't believe in writer's block is like saying you don't believe in the existence of squirrels, or emotions, or thoughts. I don't think there's any debate on the existence of squirrels… is there? Clearly thoughts and emotions exist because the vast majority of us experience them constantly (with only very few, specific exceptions). I think that when people say they don't believe that writer's block exists, what they really mean is that they believe it is always possible to overcome it. I tend to agree with that.

If you are experiencing stress over your inability to make progress on your manuscript, then try writing something completely different and silly just to break the block. I'm a big fan of writing a list of the most entertaining swear words I can think of in order to break a block. It works! It's about being light-hearted with language, it takes away the tension (I'm 99.9% sure that's how the term "cockwomble" was coined).

If you want some more serious advice then try writing flash fiction (a very short story of under 1000 words) or in a totally different genre. Try journaling to sort through your thoughts. This goes for whatever is causing you stress or keeping you in survival mode. Getting your thoughts down on paper or typing them up, can help you to organise them and overcome the negative ones.

I write Morning Pages. This concept was introduced to the world by Julia Cameron in her book The Artist's

Way. The idea is to write three pages by hand first thing in the morning, just stream of consciousness. I splurge my dreams, my feelings, what I did the previous day, my problems, my aspirations - whatever comes to mind as I write. I swear by this form of journaling for sorting through my complex thoughts and feelings. It has helped me to come unstuck many times. It declutters my head, ready for the day ahead. If you're feeling stuck, I suggest giving this a try.

Creativity

Doing anything creative that you enjoy is a key component of overcoming stress and anxiety. We all need creativity in our lives. Unplanned, motiveless creativity undertaken with abandon. In the words of the marvellous Ray Bradbury "Don't think. Thinking is the enemy of creativity. It's self-conscious, and anything self-conscious is lousy. You can't try to do things. You simply must do things." If you're limping along in survival mode and can't see any way to move forward on your goals, please carve out some time to be creative just for fun.

Why else might you be stuck with your goals?

You Don't Have Time

We've all been there. We've all longed for great big, open stretches of time just to write. Sometimes we tell ourselves we can ONLY write with such spaces. Even Herman Melville felt as though he didn't have enough time to write. He wrote in a letter to his friend, Nathaniel Hawthorne, that he couldn't finish his book because, "I am so pulled hither and thither by circumstances."

But I'm going to hit you with some tough love – suck it up. Melville still managed to finish *Moby Dick*, and you can finish your book too. We'll deal with the "not enough time" issue later in the book, mainly by ditching the busy work and focusing on your priorities. But suffice it to say, it's an excuse that you put in your own way, and it's time to let it go.

Real Talk: Maybe You're Doing it Wrong?

We all set the wrong goals at some time or another. Or we fail to take the appropriate action to achieve those goals. That's where this book will help! We're going to get into how to set the right goals and take the right steps towards accomplishing them.

Don't beat yourself up over it. I spent years getting it

wrong, and I'm a work in progress too.

Have a think about your past goals now and look critically at them. Were they realistic? Did they fit in with your life? Were they things you could control? It's okay if you answered no. You're here now and I can help get you on track.

 Exercise - Check In With Your Life Right Now

Have a look at your life and do a stock take:

Are you in crisis or survival mode? Are you just coming out of either?

_____

_____

_____

_____

What steps can you take to reduce the stress in your life?

_____

_____

_____

_____

_____

_____

_____

_____

_____

What goals have you set in the past and what stopped you from achieving them? Be honest with yourself. The process of improving this area of your life begins now and can only happen if you do the work. Don't restrict yourself to writing goals. Look at your whole life; it's all connected. Maybe you're a really effective goal setter in one area of your life but not in others. Look for weak links and let's work through them together.

_____

_____

_____

_____

_____

_____

_____

_____

_____

Chapter 2: What's Your Character's Motivation?

What is your big why?

The very first step to effective goal setting is to get in touch with your big why.

Why do you want to write? Why do you want to publish? Why have you chosen the publishing path that you have? What fires you up and gets your creative juices flowing?

Taking some time to think about the answers to these questions can help to frame the goals you set yourself, and keep you motivated. Your big why might take the form of a goal, but it doesn't have to. In some ways it may be better if it doesn't.

For example, your big why might be, "To financially

support my family". With some tweaking, which we'll come to in the next chapter, this would make a good goal. But your big why might equally be something like, "Because if I don't write the demons in my head will drive me crazy." I'm not judging. That's more or less my big why. It's definitely not a goal. Unless we re-frame it to be a mental health goal.

The problem with having a goal as your big why is that you may need to find another one when you achieve it. Of course, there's nothing wrong with that. But it may not be the right answer to motivate you during tough times if it's something that isn't permanent. If it's not a feeling deep within your soul, it might not be there when you need to call on it.

"To have a bestseller" is a solid goal to aim for, but will that thought really comfort you during a bout of writer's block, or when crisis mode strikes? What about once you have that bestseller? What will motivate you then? Chances are, that's not your real why. Go deeper. Why do you want to have a bestseller? Always peel back the layers to get to the true why behind everything else.

"To entertain a huge number of readers". Why? "Validation tells me that I'm not wasting my time". Why is that important? "Because knowing that people love my book helps to keep me going" THERE! So your why might really be, "To entertain/move/inspire people with my writing". That's why you really do it. You could almost certainly dig even deeper with that example.

It's a bit like psychoanalysis. But as I am not a qualified psychotherapist I won't attempt to analyse you. This is simply an exercise for you to try in order to find that core reason for what you're doing.

What does success look like to you?

No one can tell you what success is. It will be different for all of us. It might be an annual income amount, or a certain number of books or sales, or it might be something a bit more nebulous, like freedom. Maybe it's the ability to work from home so that you can be there to pick up your child from school, or to be able to travel the world and work wherever you are.

Think about the people you admire and what their life may look like. Is that something you want to emulate? Or is there an alternative lifestyle that you aspire to? Perhaps you see the popular definition of success and feel as though it completely misses the mark for you. Is success really about bank balances, international travel and accolades? Or is it having a little house off the grid for your family to enjoy peace and a slower pace of life?

It's a good idea to think about this when trying to work out your big why. Those hopes and dreams can form the basis of a plan.

What are your values?

In addition to finding the answer to "why do you want to write?", you should also take some time to consider what your core values are. What do you want to stand for? What are the stilts that your entire life stand upon? This might come down to a single word, or a few of them. If you've seen the excellent Disney Pixar film *Inside Out*, your values are like Riley's "islands" in her head. They are the aspects of her personality that make her who she is and define what's important to her. For example, she has "family", "hockey", and "goofball" islands made up of her memories of those things. If you don't know what I'm talking about, then you have my permission to put this book down for a couple of hours to go and find out.

My primary core value is "freedom". In all areas of my life, this is what I am striving towards, it's the thing I want to cultivate more than anything else. It affects my writing, my business, my parenting, my relationships, and how I spend my time.

Yours can be anything and should come fairly quickly to you. You'll know what matters most to you, even if you haven't framed it in these terms before. For example, perhaps you're a political activist and believe passionately in "equality". Or maybe you're a teacher, academic, or lifelong learner and prize "education". If you always have the wellbeing of your "family" at the forefront of your mind when making decisions, then there you go. Start to think about these core values now. Don't force it. If nothing comes to you straight away, sit with the idea for a while. Try journaling on it, or writing a list and then narrowing it down to just a few words.

Why does it matter?

Your big why will help you to understand which goals you should be aiming for. If it's financial security that drives you, your goals need to be focused on maximising income and making it as secure as possible.

If it's a desire to quiet the voices in your head, your goals are better off being centred on maximising writing time.

Whatever your big why, it will frame all of the goals you set going forward. Just as you need to know what motivates the characters in your fiction so that you can make their behaviour consistent and relatable, you need to know your own motivation in order to develop consistent and effective habits and behaviours that will allow you to reach your goals.

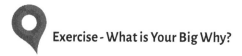 **Exercise - What is Your Big Why?**

Ask yourself these questions in order to discover your big why:

Why do you write? Try a few ideas on for size and don't forget to peel back the layers.

_____

_____

_____

_____

_____

_____

_____

_____

What does success look like to you?

_____

_____

_____

_____

_____

_____

_____

_____

What are your core values?

_____

_____

_____

_____

_____

_____

_____

Can you encapsulate your Big Why in a single sentence?

_____

_____

_____

Exercise - Make it Tangible

- *Create a mood board.*

Head to Pinterest, Canva, or search the internet for images that represent what matters most to you. It could be pictures of beautiful houses, stacks of cash, far flung travel destinations, a comfortable on-screen balance of a savings account, your dream office, someone you want to collaborate with some day, or anything else that came up when you thought about what motivates you.

Once you have your big why mood board, put it somewhere that you can see it easily. If it's a Pinterest board, make sure you have the app on your phone and pick a time of day to look through the board – don't allow notifications to distract you! Print out a collage and put it up near to where you do your writing, or somewhere around your home that you'll see it often. I have a collection of pictures taped on the inside of my wardrobe door so I see it every day when I get dressed. I also have a Pinterest board that I look at most days.

Chapter 3: Get SMART

"Goals are dreams with deadlines."

— Diana Scharf Hunt

What are SMART Goals?

Throughout this book, I'm going to be sharing with you the goal setting techniques that I use and that others have found invaluable.

At the heart of my entire goal setting process are SMART goals. For those unfamiliar with the concept, SMART is an acronym to help you to make goals that have the best chance of being accomplished.

SMART goals are:
>Specific
>Measurable
>Attainable
>Realistic
>Time-bound

The concept is used across all sorts of industries, from corporate to creative. It's a popular technique because it works. Before I discovered SMART goals, I floundered around, setting the same, vague and unhelpful goals for myself. I started to make real progress when I learned how to set SMART goals. I'll break down each part of the acronym now and get to why this technique is so effective.

Specific

Goals should be narrowed down and precise. We're not settling for, "write a book". We need to think along the lines of "write a book of approximate length x, in [genre] and [sub-genre], for y market". A business goal that is specific might be, "update About page and Books page on website with latest info", or "break into foreign rights markets with French and German translations and x invested into targeted ads".

Get granular here. The more specific, the better. Vague goals are less likely to be achieved because time passes and you have nothing to focus on. This is why I'm not a fan of New Year's Resolutions. They tend to take the form of goals like, "lose weight", "go to the gym more", or "write a book". Without a specific destination and a plan of how to get there, they're not likely to be achieved. Most resolutions are forgotten by February. Their lack of specificity is a big part of the reason they fall by the wayside.

Keep your big why in mind when picking a specific goal. You know what motivates you, so how are you going to get there? What's the first step along the way? If you're aiming for freedom, then what income goal do you need in order to establish that freedom lifestyle? How many books do you need to sell to get there? How are you going to sell those books? What's your market? Where are they?

I know I just threw a lot of questions at you, but you need to consider them all when coming up with the set of specific goals that will get you closer to your big why. It's very likely that you will need multiple specific goals; we'll get more into how to break down large projects and set goals throughout the year later in the book. For now, just think about how you can get as specific as possible each time you set a goal.

Measurable

How do you know if you've reached your goal? As well as making it specific, make it measurable. Your book's word count will be dependent, in part, on genre and market conventions. I can't say I've ever accurately predicted the word count of a book before I wrote it. It's as long as it needs to be. But perhaps you could add the goal of writing a certain number of words per day, or per writing session, until your story is finished.

If it's a sales goal or income goal, put a number on it so

that you know how you're progressing. If you want to earn £20,000 in a year from sales, make sure you know your royalty rate and how many books you need to sell to reach that target. A little maths now will help you to accomplish that income goal. You'll be able to work out how many sales per month, week, or day will get you to that annual target. This will help you to assess marketing strategies and enable you to adapt to challenges and successes.

If you don't include numbers in your goal, it'll be too vague and too hard to track your progress towards it. In my experience, this is the main place people go wrong. They create a pretty specific goal, but don't put a way to measure it in place, so there's no way of monitoring progress and making suitable tweaks to strategy.

As well as word count and sales, you can measure time spent on a project; number of reviews; number of subscribers; or number of social media posts per week. This list is far from exhaustive. When thinking about your goal, if there is nothing about it that can be measured, it isn't a SMART goal. Think again. Is there a different angle to approach it from?

If your specific goal is related to ad spend, you can measure and track this by specifying your budget and the click rate you want to achieve. As a general rule, when advertising your books you'll want to start with a small budget and gradually scale up. You can measure that scaling process and the results you get.

The main point I want to emphasise here is that having a measurable aspect to your goal will help you achieve it because you'll be able to see quite clearly if you're getting closer or not. If something isn't working, you can adjust your strategy and tweak things until you do start making progress. But with nothing to measure, you can't be adaptable in that way.

"Go to the gym more" may bring the illusion of flexibility, but it also gives your subconscious an easy way out. "Well, you didn't say how often..." you tell yourself when you realise it's been three months since you last went. But "Go to the gym for 45 minutes three times a week" has far less wriggle room. If you find yourself not sticking to it, then you can look at why, and make changes. It might mean changing the goal – that happens. Life can force you to reassess your goals and we'll get into more detail on that later. If you aren't measuring anything though, you may not realise that you need to re-evaluate your goal in the first place.

Attainable

Is the goal realistic from where you are now? Have a look back at previous goals you've set yourself. Did you achieve them, or fall short? What has previous performance been like? If you've never finished a novel before, or written at a pace of one book every two years, is it attainable to set a goal of writing six books this year? Look at the time you have available and your life circumstances. Consider what other factors will affect your ability to accomplish your goal.

Make sure that you take all of this into consideration and set a goal that you can reasonably achieve. Otherwise it'll just be another forgotten New Year's Resolution.

This can be the trickiest part of setting a SMART goal. It requires pragmatism and for your boss brain to override your creative one, who still thinks it can go from earning pennies to millions in six months if you just hit the right spot of luck.

You absolutely should have "Oprah-sized" dreams if that's what you want. But getting there will need to be done in increments. There's no point setting yourself up to fail with an unattainable goal in the beginning. If you fall short, disappointment can hold you back and slow you down. So what are the steps towards that ultimate dream? Break it down and call it a five- or ten-year plan. Then draw a map to get there.

If you want a seven-figure business and are starting from scratch, what can you do this year to get to four or five figures? Then how will you scale up?

Setting a smaller goal now doesn't mean you lack ambition, it just means you're being SMART.

Relevant

Is your goal pushing you towards your big why? Now do you see why I got you to think about that? All of the smaller goals you set need to be moving towards that dreamy goal, that lifestyle that you're aspiring towards.

Something can be specific, measurable, and attainable, but if it's ultimately pointless in relation to your big why, it's a waste of your time and effort. If your big why is to win awards and be pals with Stephen King, then becoming an indie author of erotica books probably isn't the right course of action.

This is why it's a good idea to have a visible reminder of your big why close at hand when setting your goals. Make sure you are always driving towards the things that inspire and motivate you.

Time-Bound

Put a deadline on it. In order for those measurable and attainable qualities to have meaning, you need an end date in mind. It could initially be non-specific, for example "this year", or "by August", and as you get closer to that target you can get more specific and put an actual date on it. But always put a time frame into your goals. Deadlines can have different effects on people, so it does depend a bit on your personality type, but as a general rule, setting an expected completion date on your goals will help you to reach them.

I find this much easier with business goals than writing goals. The writing doesn't always cooperate, especially when life throws unexpected things at you. We looked at ways to deal with this in the first chapter, so refer back to that if you ever feel stuck.

Deadlines are implicit in some goals. For instance, an annual income goal is obviously what you intend to earn in a given calendar or financial year – pick one definition of a year and stick to it. Other goals need to be capped so they don't drag out. "Get 10,000 email subscribers" is open-ended. By when? 20 years from now? There's no rush or impetus to take action on that. "Get 10,000 new subscribers in 12 months" has a deadline and you know you can't hang around and wait. You have to be proactive and go get those subscribers.

Giving yourself a deadline puts that pressure on that will drive you to take action. If you're someone who rebels against deadlines, you may need to get sneaky with yourself! Find ways to trick yourself into setting deadlines without putting hard dates on things. This is where accountability can really help. If you announce on social media that your new book will be out in two months, then you'd better follow through. Without a fixed date, though, you've been flexible enough that you have room to rebel just a little. The first of the month or the last of the months is still within that time, right?

Let's take a look at an example SMART writing goal:

> Write a 100,000 word noblebright epic fantasy
> novel in 9 months.

This is <u>specific</u>: you've put numbers on it (let's assume here that you've paid close attention above and already have a history of writing books of this length within this sort of timeframe) and defined the genre.

It's <u>measurable</u>: you can track your word count.

It's <u>attainable</u>: you have a record of writing at this pace.

It's <u>relevant</u>: if your big why is to publish a book a year, or any number of other dreams.

It's <u>time-bound</u>: you're going to complete it within 9 months.

Here's an example of a SMART business goal:

> Increase earnings by 20% to £20,000 from 7408
> book sales in 2020.

It's <u>specific</u>: you have a defined target and parameters.

It's <u>measurable</u>: you can track your revenue and sales numbers.

It's <u>attainable</u>: you're only aiming for a 20% increase on the previous year.

It's <u>relevant</u>: if your big why is an income goal, financial stability, freedom etc.

It's <u>time-bound</u>: it's an annual income goal for the current calendar year.

Is Your Writing Goal Attainable for the kind of writer you are?

It's worth taking a moment to consider what kind of writer you are: how quick and consistent are you? If you take a year or more to write a book, are you happy with that output, or would you like to speed it up? Getting quicker could be a goal in itself. Or if you write quickly, is that sustainable long-term, or do you need to take breaks in between projects?

Do you write every single day? Or do you fit your writing in around another job that requires you to just write on your days off? Some people will go away for a long weekend and write a huge amount away from distractions, and then write nothing for a month.

So, what's your style?

Consistent Constance

You write your words every day. You've mastered routines and never waver. You're probably an early riser and put your words first, hitting that word count goal before most people are even awake. Over time you've increased your output from a few dozen words before breakfast to maybe a few thousand before you turn to anything else.

Binge-and-Fast Betty

You churn out tens of thousands of words in a matter of days or weeks. You've won NaNoWriMo at least once, if not regularly. When you're in drafting mode, everything else becomes background noise and you fly through your words. When you're done, you skid to a halt and pause the writing to catch up on other things for a while before returning for another cycle.

Reliable Richard

You're a regular, but not daily, writer. Your schedule limits when you can write, so you fit your words into pockets of time. Weekends and days off are writing gold and you can get through a lot of words in those intervals. Perhaps you favour writing retreats once every couple of months and that's when you get most of your words written.

Sporadic Spencer

You don't particularly track when or how much you write, and have no set timetable or routine, but somehow words appear! You can't quite account for it, but you always have words to show for your effort.

Whatever kind of writer you are, account for it in your goal setting. If you're a Sporadic Spencer and quite happy that way, there's no point setting a goal of writing 2000 words every day. If you're a Consistent Constance but your output is limited to one good-length novel a year, it's not realistic to plan to write and publish six full-length novels a year – maybe build up to that.

What might Betty set as a SMART goal to help her reach her big why of financial freedom? She's not likely to be able to release a book every month year-round. Instead, she might set something like:

> Publish 3 books in 2020; a trilogy of YA urban fantasy with a focus on getting a high read through of 40%.

It's specific: 3 books, a defined genre and market, and a marketing strategy of driving read through, with a specific target in mind.

It's measurable: Betty can track her book count and read through rate. (Read through is the number of people who read book one and go on to read books two and three.)

It's <u>attainable</u>: Betty's capable of writing a full-length book in about 6 weeks, and can do that several times a year.

It's <u>relevant</u>: Betty's why is financial freedom, which is more attainable with a bigger backlist and a deep series.

It's <u>time-bound</u>: Betty has a one-year plan.

Exercise

What kind of writer are you?

_____

_____

Would you prefer to become a different kind of writer?

_____

_____

Set yourself one SMART goal.

_____

_____

_____

_____

Chapter 4: The Hero's Journey AKA Make a Plan

"OUR GOALS CAN ONLY BE REACHED THROUGH A VEHICLE OF A PLAN, IN WHICH WE MUST FERVENTLY BELIEVE, AND UPON WHICH WE MUST VIGOROUSLY ACT. THERE IS NO OTHER ROUTE TO SUCCESS."

— Pablo Picasso

Now that we've covered what SMART goals are and how they might look for a writer, we're going to get into how you might plan out your goals over a year (or more).

Start Big

We looked at coming up with your big why and how that will determine the rest of your goals. So, if you haven't done that yet, I highly recommend you pause reading for a few minutes to figure this out. Everything that we cover in the rest of this chapter will hinge on you knowing your big why. We're essentially going to work backwards from that in order to construct a plan for how to get to where you want to go.

Do you have your big why neatly defined in a single sentence? Have you created some sort of visual representation of it? Even if that's just writing it on a sticky note and sticking it to the front of your planner, or on the edge of your computer screen.

If your big why is a goal already, then you're all set. If your big why is something like "Freedom", or "to keep the demons at bay", then we have an extra layer of goal setting to do. There's absolutely nothing wrong with that. As I mentioned previously, this is in some ways preferable. You can keep your why indefinitely and adjust your goals accordingly, rather than having to rethink your big why every time you reach a goal.

So, thinking long-term, what do you want your life to look like in five years? That "freedom" that motivates you, what does it look like? What sorts of things did you put on your vision board for it?

We're going to turn that dream into a SMART goal. Dreams are great, but make it a plan and you stand a much better chance of making it a reality. So let's get Specific, Measurable, Attainable, Relevant, and Time-bound.

If your big why is something more like "to keep the demons in my head quiet", I want you now to think about a long-term plan for your life and set your big why to one side briefly. We'll come back to it, it'll help inform most of your goals, but for now we're going to focus on more tangible things.

If you've dreamt of a certain lifestyle for a while now, then this probably won't be too difficult; if you've rarely thought past next week before now, this may be more of a challenge.

Consider your values: what things are important to you that you want to cultivate more of in your life? For example, my core values are freedom, community, and equality. So my five-year plan incorporates these values, and the lifestyle I'm striving for exemplifies them.

It could be that your long-term idea is more specific already, for instance, "to have published twenty books". That's great too. I'm not here to tell you what you should or shouldn't be striving towards. It might be a lifestyle, or an accolade, or a financial goal, or it could be something else entirely. We're all creative people here, so the only limit is your imagination.

Even though I've asked you to turn this into a SMART goal, keep it long-term and overarching at this point. We're going to dig down shortly.

A five-year SMART goal might look something like this:

> Generate an annual income of £150,000 from books, sponsorships (on podcast and YouTube), Patreon, courses, and affiliate marketing within the next five years.

It's <u>specific</u>: Income and revenue sources are defined.

It's <u>measurable</u>: Income from each source can be tracked.

It's <u>attainable</u>: Starting from annual income of £15,000, with a backlist and pipeline, accountability partners, and a solid 30 hours a week to work on this.

It's <u>relevant</u>: Financial freedom is the why.

It's <u>time-bound</u>: 5 years to achieve the target.

Exercise

What is your long-term SMART goal?

_____

_____

_____

_____

_____

_____

_____

_____

How are you going to get there?

You might now be feeling pumped up and excited to break this down, or you might be feeling overwhelmed. There is no right or wrong. If you feel overwhelmed, take a deep breath, and don't panic. We're going to break this down together.

Large projects require systems, smaller sub-projects, and task lists in order to get them done. Your long-term plan is a grand project. Just as renovating a house requires planning and dividing into smaller steps along the way, so does your long-term plan.

What smaller steps will you take on the way to your ultimate goal? If you defined a number of books, or an income level in the last step, then break that down into numbers for each year in order to meet your deadline. I used the example of five years in the last section because that's a good amount of time to be working towards some significant changes and aspirations, yet not so long that it feels distant and unattainable. You can put whatever time frame you want on your goal. Think about that now and figure out how much progress you need to make each year in order to get there.

If it's an income goal, remember that income growth tends to be exponential, rather than linear. If you want to make it to six figures in five years, it's unrealistic to expect to make one fifth of it this year, then another fifth next year, and so on. Your growth is unlikely to go up by the same amount each year. It's more likely that your income will start low and growth will accelerate. So in year four you may still be on a mid five-figure revenue, £50,000 or so, before it explodes in the final year and you sail past the £100,000 mark. I might plan to go from zero to six figures in this way:

Year one: 5,000

Year two: 12,000

Year three: 25,000

Year four: 50,000

Year five: 100,000

That's just one possible projection, and something to bear in mind.

If your goal revolves around a certain number of books, and you currently write one book every two years, build up to multiple books per year rather than expecting to do it straight away. Aim for one this year, two next year, three the year after, and so on. Think exponential.

Again, these steps need to be SMART. Plan out the annual steps you're going to take to get to that long-term goal. It may be the case that your long-term goal is more complex, requiring thought to be given to each aspect of it.

For example, if your big why is "freedom" and your five-year plan is to be earning x amount so that your partner can leave their job and you can move to a bigger house in another country (great plan, by the way) you'll need to make sure you have SMART goals that address each part of that, and build up the lifestyle that you're aspiring to. Each year you'll need to have milestone goals that will get you there within your time frame.

As long as your long-term goal is also a well thought out SMART goal, this shouldn't be a problem or require too much extra planning. A solid SMART goal is the best foundation for all of this.

We need to touch back on that big why here. Those personal values and your overriding motivation for what you're doing will be strong factors in figuring out what your long-term goal is and what the best steps are to get there. If you write to purge the demons, maybe you aren't chasing a huge income or freedom lifestyle. Maybe your long-term goal is centred on your mental health, or simply having the time and freedom to do the writing. If so, it might be the case that you have no interest in turning your writing into a business and you plan to keep your day job, or generate a passive income from something else entirely, freeing you up to write in your spare time.

Plan your goals around what matters to you and what will fulfil you and feed your big why.

Exercise

Break down your long-term plan into manageable pieces. What milestones do you need to meet each year on the way to your long-term deadline?

_____

_____

_____

_____

_____

_____

_____

_____

_____

_____

_____

_____

_____

_____

_____

_____

_____

Let's Plan Out This Year

So now you know what you need to accomplish this year in order to get you closer to your long-term goal. How will you manage it? It's time to break the year into quarters and repeat the steps above.

It's probably the case at this point that you need to start setting other sub-goals in order to get you to your specific annual and long-term goals. How are you going to reach that income level, or that number of books?

Think about how much time you have available to dedicate to working on this goal. Be honest and realistic about it.

Again, it's best to work backwards: think about what you want to achieve by the end of the twelve-month period, be it a calendar year, financial year, or just the 12 months from the day you picked up this book.

What will you be best working on in the final quarter of that period? And the third, second, and first? Take it in logical steps and think about any factors that are likely to affect how each quarter goes. Plan for being able to do less work around Christmas, for example, or in the summer holidays if you have kids normally in school or are going travelling. Do you participate in National Novel Writing Month in November? Or the Camp iterations in April and July? If so, factor that into your writing schedule for the year.

If you set an income goal, then just as with the five-year plan, be aware that growth is unlikely to be linear. You are unlikely to make a quarter of your total in quarter one, for instance. You might want to plan to make as much as half of it in the final quarter, although this will depend on your time line.

With book sales, be mindful of the drop off a certain period after a new book launches. Don't be deterred, simply plan your year with this in mind, and remember that you can drive sales to your backlist with good marketing strategies. You might also want to plan a launch strategy that compensates for this drop off, for instance, releasing a book every month, or every six weeks for a period of the year.

I am not suggesting you write and publish a book every month, certainly if that's not the norm for you, but you may want to hold off on publishing a book you recently finished so that you can release the sequel, or a second stand-alone, soon afterwards. This is known as "rapid releasing" and is a strategy that a lot of writers swear by.

Releasing high quality products is essential if you want to earn a good living with integrity, so I don't advocate rushing anything, but timing your launches strategically can be an important factor in your income.

You may find that with any given title, you get the opposite of a snowball, with the majority of the royalties being earned in the first month after launch. You then need to factor in the delay in receiving those royalties. It will be 60-90 days after a sale that you actually get the money, unless you sell a lot of your books directly from your website.

Be consistent with how you log your income. You may want to count your revenue when it's earned, or wait until it's received. It's up to you how you do this, but be consistent with how you log your income.

If you provide any services or courses where you receive a payment up front, then there's a delay in when you provide the content. Again, be consistent in your record-keeping.

If you offer a course with a payment plan, you'll need to plan for a certain percentage of cancelled or failed payments, and price in a way that enables you to cope with that loss.

As in the example I gave above of a five-year goal, you may have other sources of income that you want to consider in your plans. You'll need to consider how much time you can dedicate to working on each individual project, and build up a schedule for the year that spreads out launches accordingly.

I'm naturally quite an impulsive person. I get shiny new object syndrome regularly and can be easily distracted from my plans by a new idea. One year I got swept up in this particularly badly, and ended up taking on a number of commitments with other people that heavily impacted my writing plans. So I now allow myself flexibility for new ideas and opportunities that may come along. Rather than denying my natural personality, it's better for me to work with it.

If that's true for you too, spread your plans out throughout the year and give yourself periods of breathing room to allow for those spontaneous side quests!

There might be an event announced that you want to attend, or the chance to collaborate with someone else, or simply a new idea for a book that captures your imagination and insists on interrupting your planned writing schedule. That actually happened to me with this very book! I had a gap in my schedule and was able to fit writing this into that gap because I had the forethought to allow for this sort of situation.

I'll go into greater detail in coping with change in a later chapter, but for now, let's just say that it's a good idea to leave spaces throughout the year to allow for both positive and negative disruptions.

What I like to do is create a spread in my business planner that is divided into quarters. I look at my desired end goal and plug the projects that will get me to that goal into the relevant quadrants.

I'm a multi-passionate person, so my projects are

diverse. Yours might not be. It might be books, books, and more books. Or it might be heavily focused on one thing, with a minor side project. All of these projects should feed into your big why, or your long-term goal.

For example, an income goal from multiple streams of income will be achieved by giving time to each of those income streams. Pick avenues that you enjoy, rather than ones you feel you ought to pursue. For God's sake, don't start a YouTube channel if you hate seeing yourself on camera. Don't create an online course if you have no interest in teaching people. Go with what your strengths are, and things that fit your big why. Perhaps challenge yourself to branch out into something new if it serves you to do so, but not at the expense of your happiness.

Take a logical approach here and sort your projects into the quarters that make sense for you. If there's something that will need a lot of planning, give it two quarters. If you know that it takes you six months to write a book, give yourself that time to write and another quarter to launch. I also recommend that you don't plan a book launch in the same month as another big launch, such as a course or an event. Having one solid focus at a time will allow you to give that project your full attention.

 Exercise

Break your year into quarters and place your projects into the relevant quarters.

Q1:

_____

_____

_____

_____

_____

_____

_____

_____

Q2:

_____

_____

_____

_____

_____

_____

_____

_____

Q3:

_____

_____

_____

_____

_____

_____

_____

Q4:

_____

_____

_____

_____

_____

_____

_____

Chapter 5: The Nitty Gritty of Your Task List

Let's Get Granular

Now that you have an overview of your year ahead, let's get into the nitty gritty of exactly what you're going to do and when. It's likely that you will have tasks that will need to be repeated throughout the year in order to meet your goals. Things such as updating and checking on your ads; setting up newsletter swaps; posting to social media; entering promotions; emailing your mailing list; and many more admin and marketing tasks.

I recommend putting anything that happens on a regular schedule, such as newsletters, in your calendar. For example, I send mine every two weeks, so I have a running record of when I'm due to send it that I can refer to for setting up promotions and newsletter swaps with other authors. When I know I have a launch date in mind, I'll add to the calendar, because I always send extra emails out around launches. I keep these free of promotions for other authors' books, however, so they don't get added in to the promo cycle.

Another thing you can add in at this stage is any deadlines around launches. For example, if you have an editor or cover designer booked for a specific date; the date you intend to send out advanced reader copies (ARCs) of your new book; any paid or unpaid promotions that you're enrolled in; and so on.

As you begin to fill out your calendar, you'll start to see which are your busier months and which are quieter. Double check now that you've given yourself enough room to manoeuvre. Have you allowed enough time for each step of the publishing process? Have you allowed for periods of rest and spontaneity?

With your quarterly goals in mind, think about what tasks are going to help you to make progress towards them during each quarter. As writers, we're going to want to put the words first almost all of the time, but what other tasks are required to move you forward? Do you need to invest time in learning anything new in order to get the best results?

For instance, if you have a revenue goal and know that you need to run ads in order to meet that goal, are you equipped with the experience and knowledge to get moving on those ads? Or do you need to invest in a coaching program first? Have you allowed for that in your plan for the year? Don't assume that you can just wing it. You can end up wasting a lot of valuable time, and potentially money, while you make mistakes before figuring it out. I found that with my goal to start a YouTube channel. I'd done a little bit of video creation and editing before and thought I would just learn as I went along, but the software I had used in the past was now obsolete. I spent days searching for replacement software that was intuitive and had just the right amount of bells and whistles for my needs. I made one video and put it up, then stalled because it had taken me so long. I still felt no closer to having the right skills or know-how to keep going.

At the time of writing this, there is still just the one video on my channel, and I've made no progress with learning what I need to know. That's in part because of how crazy the world has been for the last few months, but I was stalled for two months before that as well. I now know that I will need to dedicate a full quarter of a year to really learn the ropes, and will need to treat that educational time as a launch period, giving it my focus and prioritising it. YouTube is still on my goals list, but it's been bumped back to a later point in time.

Be realistic about how much time your projects will require as you lay out your plans for the year ahead. Look at your goals for the year, and each quarter, and make lists of the launches, projects, and areas of focus that you will need to give time to in order to meet those goals. Finishing a certain number of books is fairly straightforward – you just need to write the words – yes, I know, often easier said than done! A revenue goal, however, may be more complicated. How are you going to reach it? How many books do you need to sell? Or are you planning for income from multiple sources, such as a monetised YouTube channel or podcast? If so, you'll need to break down each income stream and make a separate plan for each of them.

Think of this process as placing stepping stones across a river in order to reach the other side. Each project is an essential step towards your goals. There is no benefit to extra side steps that don't get you closer to the other bank. Make sure every one of your intended projects does move you closer to a goal. That's not to say that you can't have recreational projects in addition to professional ones. I set personal goals regularly and spend time working on advancing those as well as my writing and publishing goals. I spend a fair amount of time just watching TV or playing games too! Don't get me wrong, that relaxation time is nourishing in many instances. But it's also important to know when it's veering into procrastination and to nip that in the bud.

With the fixed blocks of your schedule accounted for in your calendar, it's time to break down each project into all of the tasks you'll need to accomplish. I do this by hand in my business planner, but you might like to use software, or a mobile app. You'll find a list of resources at the back of this book detailing all the handy tools I've found over the years.

Whatever planning system works best for you, now is the time to crack it open and use it. Create a page, document, or list for each project, and brainstorm all of the tasks that need to be done in order to complete that project. For writing and publishing a book, this is going to include writing the first draft, revising it, hiring an editor (possibly two depending on if you need developmental as well as copy edits), hiring a cover designer, researching keywords and categories, scheduling beta readers, deciding on a pricing strategy, formatting the final manuscript, and finally hitting publish. Then you have all of the marketing and advertising to do. Deep breaths. You're okay, this is a lot, but it is all totally doable with a thorough plan.

You might want to break up writing the book, prepping it for launch, and launching it into three separate projects to make it all seem less overwhelming. The chances are, these three stages are going to take up at least two quarters of the year, if not more, so it might make sense to break it up this way.

Once you have your projects broken down into their component tasks, you can decide what is achievable in the time you have. It might now be clear that you need to allow more time for some things, and perhaps less for others.

Around your big blocks of fixed appointments, deadlines, launches, and so on, you're going to pick out your tasks for your projects and fit them into your work hours (or leisure hours if writing is a hobby, or if you have recreational or personal goals).

If you didn't believe me earlier when I said you need a plan for your goals, I hope you can see it now!

It will be helpful to save the task lists you write as templates for future projects, to save you from having to re-write them each time.

Planning Guide

We've covered a lot of ground here and I've thrown a lot at you. But I know you can handle it! To help get you started, I've created a bundle of planning worksheets that you can print and use in a planner, or with a calendar to plan out your year. You can get a PDF copy at https://www.subscribepage.com/goalsettingforwriters.

 **Exercise**

Using my PDF guide and a planner, calendar, or notebook, pick your first major project and create a task list of everything you need to do in order to complete that project.

If you feel as though you're on a roll, do the same for another project.

Batching

For those repetitive and regular tasks, I highly recommend setting aside some time to batch them. You will save yourself so much time in the long run if you learn how to group like tasks together and do them in bulk.

Every time you switch between different types of tasks, it takes your brain a bit of time to catch up. Different parts of your brain are used for writing, administration, communication, and marketing. If you can stick with one type of task over a longer period, say half a day, you'll waste less time switching between them and having to wait for your brain to catch up.

Tasks that I benefit from batching are: creating social media posts, signing up for promos, arranging newsletter swaps, and answering emails. I also schedule time to log in to sites like BookFunnel and my Amazon Ads dashboard. It can be all too tempting to constantly check our various dashboards for the latest data, but 99 times out of a hundred, there is nothing actionable to be achieved when we gather that data. It's far better to just look at it once a month, or once a week. Otherwise it's just a distraction.

Decide which tasks you can batch, or better yet, consider what can be dropped or outsourced, in order to free up some of your time and energy. No matter how focused we are on goals that move us forwards, when it comes to running a business there will always be tasks that need doing that are tedious and time consuming. There are things that we simply aren't that skilled at and it can sometimes make sense to give them to someone else. Make sure you know which tasks absolutely have to be done by you, like writing your next book. Then pick out things that can be outsourced. If you are in a position to hire a freelancer to do these tasks, then go for it! Take it off your plate so that you can focus your energy on the parts of your author career that you enjoy.

You probably already know that it's important to hire a professional editor and cover designer, but you can also hire social media managers, formatters, and personal assistants to pick up some of your admin.

If you aren't able to pay for freelancers, do you have a friend or family member who might use their skills for free to help you? Try asking. The worst that can happen is they turn you down. You might be surprised how willing people are to help, so ask.

If you're absolutely certain that you're on your own, then it's even more important to categorise all of your tasks and batch them.

Once you have your list of batchable tasks that you need to do, plug in some sessions in which to accomplish those tasks. Fit them into realistic places in your schedule. Be sure to account for the times when you get the most writing done and leave those times untouched! Don't schedule admin for when your creative brain is most alive. Words first! Not necessarily first thing in the morning – not all of us are at our most creative at that time – but prioritise your writing when determining your schedule; fit other tasks into other periods of time.

If you can dedicate a block of time once or twice a month to batches of repetitive tasks, it will save you time in the long run. Schedule these blocks ahead of time, so you know when they are happening. For instance, you might block out a morning in the first week of the month to set up new ads, and another block in the third week to check their status and make adjustments. You might also block out a few hours to create all of your social media posts for the month.

Investing that time up front will take it off your plate for the rest of the month and stop it from cluttering your planner, your desk, or your mental real estate.

Exercise

Which tasks can you batch?

_____

_____

_____

Which tasks can you outsource?

_____

_____

_____

Which tasks can you scrap?

_____

_____

_____

Download your free planning guide here:
subscribepage.com/goalsettingforwriters

A Note on Traditional Publishing

It may be the case that one of your goals is to get a publishing deal. I just want to address this briefly. This is not an avenue that has ever appealed to me, so I can't advise on taking this route, but what I can say is that it may be difficult to turn this into a SMART goal because it is largely outside of your control. You could make a set of SMART goals for pitching a certain number of agents, building a viable author platform (a website, a social media following, a mailing list - which many publishers expect these days) and honing your craft by reading a certain number of books on the topic and putting in a certain number of hours of writing practice. But that is about all you can control. You cannot guarantee that if you follow a certain process, you will have a publishing contract within a fixed time frame. The industry simply doesn't work like that.

It's also impossible to set your own timeline for the publication of a traditionally published book. You shouldn't expect to be receiving royalty cheques within a year of starting your first draft. Even if you manage to secure a contract, the wheels of that machine move far more slowly than in indie publishing. It could be up to two years before your completed manuscript is in book stores, so please factor this into your goal setting if this is the path you want to pursue.

Chapter 6: Kick Ass & Take Names - How To Actually Achieve Your Goals!

"In the long run, we shape our lives, and we shape ourselves. The process never ends until we die. And the choices we make are ultimately our own responsibility."

—Eleanor Roosevelt

How to Accomplish Your Goals!

So, you have a schedule for the year, you have a task list for your next project, you have blocks of time set aside for batching tasks. This is your roadmap! It's your completely unique plan for accomplishing your goals. How does it feel?

Now, how do you make sure that these tasks get crossed off and that you actually accomplish your goals?

It's the eternal question, and certainly a common one when I poll my followers on social media on the subject.

In this chapter, we're going to cover some general tips for Getting Shit Done, and I'll share the things that I have found the most useful.

Rewards

I'm a big fan of intrinsic motivation. It's something I'm trying hard to instil in my kids. I don't want them to grow up to be the sorts of people who need to reward themselves for every little thing they achieve. However, if, like many people, you grew up with sticker charts, gold stars, and promises of trips to the sea side if you did especially well at something, chances are you will benefit from rewarding yourself.

Rewards can be hugely motivating! Set yourself a series of rewards for the steps along the way to reaching your goals.

People trying to lose weight, for example, often find the promise of new clothes at certain size intervals on their way down to their ideal weight a very effective way to meet those milestones. Writers may be motivated by the opportunity to buy new stationery, or a piece of cake at every 20,000 word interval.

When I won NaNoWriMo in 2018, I planned out my rewards for every 10k I wrote and I put them into a spread in my bullet journal next to my word count tracker. Knowing that I was working towards something more tangible than a sense of pride, or bragging rights, really helped. I flew past each of my 10k milestones, hitting 50,000 words on day 18.

I've taken a great deal of pleasure in each of the rewards I earned myself that month, from a new set of colouring pencils, to a purple ukulele! Well, why not?

Whatever your goal, having milestones along the way that you intend to celebrate is a great way to build momentum for when things feel difficult. Just have the stepping stones at reasonable intervals, and pick rewards that are meaningful to you.

Pick things that you would do, or buy anyway, but deny yourself them until you reach that milestone. For example, if you're especially partial to a coffee from a particular coffee shop, tell yourself you can't have another one until you get to the halfway mark on a project. Picking rewards that you were already planning helps to prevent you overspending, but it's also something you already want. You aren't having to use creative energy choosing rewards.

Track Progress

This is implicit in the above tactic. In order to know if you're at the point at which you have earned a reward, you need to be tracking your progress. This shouldn't be a problem, as all of the goals you set yourself were SMART goals. Right? Remember, the M stands for Measurable.

Word count is the obvious one for us, but it could be monthly income or profit; it could be number of clients if you do freelance work; it could be number of sales, or number of hours spent working on a project.

If your goal is SMART, there is an element to track. Do it in a very visible way – perhaps in a bullet journal spread, or on a whiteboard above your desk: track it somewhere you will see it every day.

Adding progress to your tracker will be something you'll feel great about, so it'll motivate you to make progress every day, or week.

That's not to say that you should give yourself a hard time if you don't make progress. We all have bad days, weeks, or even months. I'm not advocating punishing yourself for that, but tracking progress is an important component of achieving goals – if you are actively working towards one, track that progress!

Vision Boards

You created a vision board for your big why at the start of this process. They can be extremely motivating, so I invite you now to create a new vision board specific to your annual goal.

Your new vision board might contain images of very literal, physical things – your own book cover, if you have one designed already, for example. It might contain a picture of a stack of cash, or a screenshot of a bank balance showing your income goal. Or your board might be more symbolic.

Focus on feelings; choose images that evoke how you want to feel at the end of the year. For example, you may want to pick colours that represent joy, excitement, security, or abundance. For instance, green and gold, unsurprisingly, represent wealth. On a vision board I made a couple of years ago I had a picture of some green agate coasters with gold rims. Not because I wanted those coasters, but because the colours and the luxurious nature of that particular item represented something for me – abundance.

You might also pick a photo of someone jumping into a lake from a high cliff to represent freedom or adventure. This will be entirely personal to you, but I encourage you to get creative and think outside of the box.

It helps to have a variety of image styles, so that your gaze doesn't skip over images. Each should be attention-grabbing and significant in its own way.

The medium you choose is entirely up to you. You might want to use Pinterest, or a folder on your computer. You might print the images out and put them on display. It's best to store the images somewhere you can easily see them every single day.

I've made the mistake before of creating image boards

and then forgetting all about them. That doesn't work. Keeping them in sight is what gives your brain the visual cue to strive to achieve that goal.

Write Them Down

"YOU CONTROL YOUR FUTURE, YOUR DESTINY. WHAT YOU THINK ABOUT COMES ABOUT. BY RECORDING YOUR DREAMS AND GOALS ON PAPER, YOU SET IN MOTION THE PROCESS OF BECOMING THE PERSON YOU MOST WANT TO BE. PUT YOUR FUTURE IN GOOD HANDS - YOUR OWN."

— Mark Victor Hansen

But, Holly, haven't I already written down my goals at least three times?

Yes, and you are going to write them down every single day. No, I'm not kidding.

You can journal them, put them in your planner or on your calendar, write them on a sticky note. Whatever you like. Go for variety in order to keep it fresh each day. Whatever medium you choose, write down your annual goal/s every day. Write them by hand. The brain internalises far more when we write by hand than when we type information. It's wizardry. But you can type them out at times as well, to mix things up.

You might even want to share them on social media. This helps with accountability (more on that in the next chapter).

Again, it's all about keeping your goals in mind as you go about your daily life. Forgotten goals go unaccomplished. Writing them down frequently keeps your attention focused on them, consistently bringing you back to the important tasks you need to complete in order to achieve that which you set out to do.

You could also set them up as reminders on your phone that show up as alerts each day. Make a separate one for each active goal, including annual, quarterly, and monthly goals. I have mixed feelings about this tip, as I also advocate turning off all notifications on your phone in order to boost productivity. However, as a mindset tactic, this can be really beneficial. Perhaps set them to appear outside of your normal working hours (assuming you keep such things, I know not all of us do!). But still make sure you write them down. Your brain likes it when you put pen to paper!

Another option is to set your computer password to something related to your primary goal for the year, so that each time you unlock your computer you are prompted to think of it. For example, if your goal is a certain revenue figure, then set your password as that figure. If your goal is to publish four books, then how about "PublishX4!"?

The idea here is to do little things that stack up throughout your day to keep your goals at the forefront of your mind.

In 2015, Dr Gail Matthews (Dominican University, California) conducted a study in which participants wrote down their goals with varying degrees of detail. Participants in one group were just asked to think about their goals. Another group wrote their goals down. Yet another also wrote down action commitments, while the fourth group also sent their action commitments to a supportive friend, and the final group regularly reported updates to that friend. Guess which group was the most successful in accomplishing their goals? People who wrote down their goals and action steps, and had an accountability system in place, were 75% more likely to succeed in their goals. So write them down. Often.

Bullet Journaling

Here's where I get a bit more personal, and slightly evangelical. If you haven't encountered the concept of a bullet journal before, I'll give you the super quick definition: it's a customisable planning system. All you need is a blank notebook and a pen to start. The system, in brief, is that you set up a page at the front of your notebook for future planning, where you allow space to write down any events, tasks, or notes for future months; you set up a monthly log with a list of all the things happening in the current or next month, depending on when you start, then create a new entry each day under which you note down in bullet points all of the tasks you need to do that day. You add to this one day at a time as a rolling task list. You then mark off completed tasks, tasks you have migrated to the next day, tasks you have delegated or scheduled for a future date, and tasks that are no longer relevant, all using a simple key. All of this is underpinned by having an index, or contents page, in the notebook. You number your pages and keep a record of what's on each page so you can easily find things again later.

I highly recommend checking out Ryder Carroll's website, and his book, *The Bullet Journal Method*, for more information.

It's a very simple system, but a whole culture and community has grown up around it. People have added to the system, and many bullet journalers add artistic embellishments. This is by no means necessary. It's perfectly fine to keep it really simple and minimal and go by the original system.

I have found this to be my number one tool for productivity and for reaching my goals. I use "collections", a term for spreads in a bullet journal that do not fit the basic logging system. I add pages to my bullet journals (I've been using this system since January 2017 and have filled a lot of notebooks!) for goal tracking.

I'm not going to give you a detailed breakdown of everything I include, as that would probably constitute an entire book in itself (uh oh, I think I just realised what my next non-fiction book will be!), but in summary, I include a 90-day goals page at the start of every new notebook, no matter when in the year I'm starting it; I add my monthly goals to each monthly overview page, and I conduct a monthly review at the end of each month in which I assess my progress.

I sometimes add other spreads, such as word count trackers, depending on what my goals are for the month. During NaNoWriMo, I almost always include a word count tracker, as well as some images to inspire the book I'm working on, and a list of rewards for each milestone.

It's completely up to you how you incorporate goal setting and tracking into your bullet journal, if you decide to use one; that's the beauty of bullet journaling, it's completely unique and customisable to you and your needs.

If you want to dive deeper into this concept, Instagram and Pinterest are beautiful sources of inspiration, but please don't be put off by the incredibly artistic images that get shared. I know people who have delayed using the system because they felt intimidated. I say again – it is okay to keep it simple.

If you would like to see how I use my bullet journal, I share spreads from my bujo on a special account on Instagram under the handle @holly.journals.

Other Planner Systems & Digital Tools

There are so many systems currently available that it's impossible to cover them all here. I just want to share a few other tools with you that I've found helpful, or that other writers I know use regularly. Whether it's a pre-printed planner, or an entirely digital system, find one that works for you and can be integrated into your life. It should be part of your routine. Think about what does and doesn't work for you, try a few things and see what sticks.

Paper Planners (other than bullet journaling)

There are so many options here that I would need to create a directory to cover them all. Take to YouTube! Check out the Happy Planner, Power Sheets, and Clever Fox. There are many more options, so try a few and see what works best for you.

Trello

This is an app for your phone, tablet, or computer that works on a list system. You create boards related to a given project, then on that board you create lists, and cards within lists. For example, for the podcast that I co-host, we have a shared board with lists for podcast topics, people to interview, hashtags to use on social media, checklists for our production process, and so on. You can re-order your lists, add attachments and images to cards, add deadlines, and all sorts of essential planning elements. It even integrates with your calendar. You can share boards with other people you collaborate with, so if you have a virtual assistant or writing partner, you can have a joint board that you use for coordinating and planning.

Some authors use Trello to plot out their books and absolutely swear by this method. I haven't used it that way myself, as I'm a discovery writer and prefer committing my notes to paper, but it's something to consider if you like digital story planning.

Trello is free. There is a paid upgrade, but so far I've got everything I needed with the free version. I like having a digital tool that is easy to use and syncs across my laptop and phone.

Scrivener

When it comes to organising your writing, there are few tools that can beat Scrivener. It's a one-stop shop for writing and researching. I'm writing these very words in it. The basic principle is that it is a supercharged word processor. There is space to write, add notes, store links and images, and more.

If you write a blog, you can do so and keep everything organised in folders within Scrivener. Likewise if you have a podcast or YouTube channel and write scripts. You could even do all of your social media planning within it. It can be used as a planner system, with folders for each goal, lists of action steps, and so on.

Scrivener's big appeal, for me personally, is the corkboard feature, which gives you a bird's-eye view of your whole project. If you use it for planning and tracking your goals, you will be able to view everything on the corkboard and see a summary of each area of focus. The cards can even be colour-coded and moved around, so you can shift priorities and reschedule things easily.

It's not a free piece of software, but a free trial is available, and the licence is relatively affordable.

Just-In-Time Learning

In the previous chapter I mentioned allowing time to learn new skills. I wanted to expand on that a bit here. I'm a big advocate of "just-in-time learning". That is, learning what you need to know, when you need to know it. In any industry there is a large volume of potentially new information which can seem daunting and overwhelming when viewed from the bottom of the mountain. But you don't need to know everything now, or even half of everything before you embark on a career as an authorpreneur. You just need to learn how to tackle each step of the climb as you come to it.

Learn how to craft a good tale first, then how to format it, then how to get it onto the retailers. You can improve your craft as you go and then dip into setting up your website and advertising. Take each new phase of your author journey as it comes and don't put pressure on yourself to become a virtuoso overnight. It isn't going to happen.

There are all sorts of resources out there for increasing your knowledge a little at a time, and many of them are free. I'd suggest the first small steps to take are to find one or two podcasts, or YouTube channels that cover topics you're interested in. Join one or two author communities where you can ask questions and get support, groups such as the Facebook community for my podcast, *Unstoppable Authors*. In the group we host writing sprint sessions, answer questions, share useful resources, and keep each other accountable. It's a really friendly and supportive community.

You might also want to join a writing critique group to get feedback on your writing. This might be a local writers' circle, or an online group. It can sometimes take a little while to find the right people, but it's worth persevering as a critique group can really help you to become a better writer.

Start slowly with your education and don't overwhelm yourself. As each skill develops, begin exploring another. There's no rush. Be strategic about what and when you learn. Pick the next thing you need to know more about and focus on it. Give yourself a month, or a quarter, to improve a certain skill or small group of related skills.

You may want to consider paid courses for more in-depth training on some topics, such as advertising, but make sure you see what you can get from that educator's free content first, and get recommendations from the author community before shelling out lots of money.

Check In Regularly

One of the main reasons I've been able to achieve the things I have is that I have a system of regular review. By now you should be on board with the idea that your goals need to be ever-present in your mind if you're going to accomplish them. Part of this process is taking the time to regularly sit down and check in with your progress.

You'll need to take some time either at the end or beginning of each week, month, and quarter to see how it's all going. This is part of my planning routine now and is second nature. Every Sunday (sometimes it gets bumped to Monday morning, let's be honest), I look back over the week in my bullet journal and see what got done and what didn't. I ask myself four questions:

1. What progress did I make towards my goals? (I focus on my monthly goals here, but may sometimes look at the long game.)

2. What did I procrastinate on and why?

3. What did I struggle with?

4. What will I do differently next week?

It doesn't take me very long to run through these questions, as I keep a daily log of what I've accomplished and what my struggles are in my bullet journal. I advocate using a day-to-day planning system that allows you to do the same. This reflection gives you an opportunity to address any problems quickly, before too much time has elapsed without progress.

At the end of every month I do a more detailed review. I check all of the stats that I track, including sales, ad spend, follower counts on social media, and income from all sources. I keep track of the same stats throughout the year, regardless of my differing goals as time passes. This way I can easily adapt and pick up slack where it appears. For example, if I see that sales on a given platform have dropped, I know I need to refocus my advertising on that platform. I'll do that even if sales are not my primary focus that month, because I always have the big picture in mind and know that a dip one month can easily lead to a long-term downward trend which would make it more difficult to then meet my sales goal in the following quarter.

This review is very much focused on metrics and data. I don't do a lot of analysis at this point. Just gather the numbers, make a record of them, and wait until you've gathered more data before you start looking for patterns.

Each quarter, then, it's time to look at the data you've

been collecting and check you're making the progress you expect. You should also check in with your gut and see if your goals still feel right. Our situations can change, life can throw unexpected things our way, so make sure that the goals you set at the start of the year are still SMART. Perhaps not all of them are relevant any more. Perhaps you started learning about something and found that it wasn't right for you, or was going to take longer than you thought, like I did with my YouTube channel. Or the opposite may have happened. Maybe you tried writing in a new genre and completely fell in love with it, so that return to your previous series in a different genre now no longer makes sense and you decide instead to pursue the new one.

If everything is ticking along exactly as planned (spoiler: it probably won't be!) then carry on as you were. Maybe stretch yourself a bit further if it seems appropriate to do so, but if, like most people, you're not seeing the progress you would have liked, it's time to take a critical look at what's going on.

We're going to go into more detail on handling obstacles later in the book, but for now, let me just say that this is absolutely normal and it's why we're doing all of this work. You weren't expecting me to say that, were you? It's not a case of do x, y and z and you will definitely fly through the year exactly as planned.

Life happens to absolutely all of us, and there are always

bumps in the road. The point of setting these goals and regularly tracking your progress is so that you are in a better position to cope when things inevitably go astray. This is why we check in regularly: so that we can adapt.

When I set out my publishing schedule for the year and lined up some outsourcing back in January 2020, I could not have predicted the massive social and political upheaval that followed. When I did my check in at the end of quarter one (and even quarter two) it wasn't yet clear just how prolonged the COVID crisis was going to be. Many of my plans have had to change and I'm guessing yours have too.

Obviously not every quarter, or even every year, features events of this magnitude, but most years will involve a birth, a bereavement, a move, or any number of other upheavals. We make our plans and then life happens.

The solution is to set plans and then review them often.

So decide how often you're going to check in, what form or forms these check ins will take, and then schedule them. Write them in your planner, or calendar, and stick to them.

Exercise

Which of the systems and tools mentioned above appeal to you the most?

_____

_____

_____

Write down some rewards to integrate into one of your SMART goals.

_____

_____

_____

_____

Decide how you're going to track your progress for the above goal.

_____

_____

_____

_____

_____

Chapter 7: Hold Yourself Accountable

"TRY HOLDING YOURSELF ACCOUNTABLE TO YOURSELF. IF YOU HAD TO GIVE YOURSELF A DAILY, WEEKLY, OR MONTHLY REPORT, WOULD YOU BE PROUD TO TALK ABOUT WHAT YOU HAD DONE, OR WOULD YOU NEED TO BE PRETTYING UP THINGS, BULLSHITTING, OR LYING TO KEEP YOUR JOB?"

— Loren Weisman

Masterminds and Accountability Groups

This handy tool for meeting your goals deserves its own chapter because it's a whopper. This is probably my number one tip for getting shit done.

Going back about four years now, I started looking for a source of community accountability. I was moving in creative business circles, as well as author circles, and was part of a couple of groups of people from all sorts of industries who all helped each other out with goal setting and accountability.

It quickly became apparent that the indie author

business is very different from other creative businesses out there, with its own special blend of advantages and challenges.

So I sought to replicate this sort of accountability community within the author world. I found a wonderful group of friends who were all at a similar stage in their careers, and we would regularly get together online to chat about our goals and how we were doing. It went beyond accountability and was a mastermind group – a space to share ideas, learn from and with each other, as well as supporting one another in our goals.

This group was so helpful and motivating, and we all learned from each other. It was an extra level of support beyond the big Facebook groups, because we were talking to each other and engaging in a true dialogue with each other. In the larger groups it can all be a bit impersonal; too many voices and not enough focus. It was the best thing that I could have done for myself at that time.

Finding a mastermind group that you can talk goals and strategy with is an important aspect for many business owners. You may find a group for people from a variety of industries that rocks your world. This option can be a great way to learn more about business generally, and give you insights into how other sectors are doing things that you can then transfer to your author business. I certainly found value in that.

A mastermind with fellow authors, however, may well be the better option, especially if you're new to the industry. It may form more of a critique group and help you learn more about the craft of writing. Or it may be more goal-oriented.

If you can't find an existing one, starting a new one is always an option. If you've been networking online, or at events with other authors, chances are you've developed a few friendships. This should be your starting point for finding new mastermind members. I advise keeping the group fairly small, no more than a dozen or so people. That way it's not too difficult to find a good time that you can all be available to talk, and it won't be too many voices and opinions crowding out any value from the exchanges.

Early in your career, I would steer clear of any paid mastermind groups, and be wary of any such groups trying to solicit your business. Later on, once you have a good income from your writing, you might want to consider a reputable, established, paid mastermind group. These can help take you to the next level in your business, but in my opinion they are absolutely not for beginners.

You might not be interested specifically in a mastermind at this point. That's absolutely fine. There are other options to get similar results. There are some absolutely wonderful groups out there for accountability. Groups where you can share what you're working towards on a regular basis, get support and encouragement and, above all, accountability.

The psychological principle is that if you have told other people, especially in a way in which there is a record, such as a social media post, then you have an extra incentive to do what you have said you will do. If you don't, you have to either go back and admit it, or stay away from the group. It's the same principle behind weight loss groups with weekly weigh-ins. You have to show your face each week and step on the scales. Even when the result is between you and the person taking your weight, you have someone else monitoring your results, and so it is an incentive to try your best.

Now, this might not work with your personality type. I certainly didn't get on with this kind of approach to weight loss, but don't assume that if this sort of system hasn't worked in one area of your life, it won't work in relation to your writing or your business.

Having the *right* group is essential. For me, I need a place that is non-judgemental, where the focus is on encouragement rather than criticism. For some, a tougher approach is welcome.

Take some time to find the right group. You could start with the group that my podcasting partner and I set up, Unstoppable Authors. We're on Facebook, and every week we share what we're working towards, what we've accomplished the previous week, and what we feel we need to do to overcome any obstacles in our way. Come and find us and share your goals with us.

Regular accountability is the key to success. Knowing that you have friends cheering you on and rooting for you can be the difference between success and falling short.

The act of writing out your goals for the week, month, quarter, and year in a semi-public way does two things: it ticks the box for writing down your goals that we talked about in the previous chapter; it also puts a gentle amount of pressure on you to do what you say you will. This accountability is highly effective for many people. It's not high pressure, because you always have the option to not return to the topic, or to show up and admit you didn't accomplish things. It's just a little nudge in the direction of productivity.

Sometimes, when I show up to report on my progress, there are things on my task list for the week that didn't get done. This is completely normal. We all experience setbacks. Even when we set realistic, achievable goals, there are times when life happens and things get in the way.

Being in an accountability group gives you the reassurance that you are not a failure when this happens. The right people around you will encourage you and help you to feel you have companions on the same journey. That's been my experience and I hope it will be yours too.

 Exercise

Find and join an accountability group (*cough* Unstoppable Authors *cough*).

Chapter 8: Overcoming the Central Conflict

"WE SHOULD STRIVE TO WELCOME CHANGE AND CHALLENGES, BECAUSE THEY ARE WHAT HELP US GROW. WITH OUT THEM WE GROW WEAK LIKE THE ELOI IN COMFORT AND SECURITY. WE NEED TO CONSTANTLY BE CHALLENGING OURSELVES IN ORDER TO STRENGTHEN OUR CHARACTER AND INCREASE OUR INTELLIGENCE."

— H.G. Wells

Handling Obstacles

In the previous two chapters, I laid out some strategies you can use to help you achieve your goals. These will make a huge difference when it's plain sailing, but as I have said several times, it's important to accept that you will encounter stormy seas sometimes.

We all experience obstacles in the journey towards achieving our goals. It's impossible to avoid them completely, and naive to think they won't slow you down. The key is to be prepared for them and account for them in your planning, which we covered in chapter four.

Having allowed time for detours and pit stops, then, how do we actually handle them when they occur?

This is an extremely personal matter. Your situation will be different from mine, or from anyone else's. Your personality, your coping strategies, and everything about your life is unique. I can't tell you what to do about every problem that may crop up in your life, but what I *can* do is lay out some of the common obstacles along with suggestions for ways to navigate around them. In researching this book, I asked several writers on social media which obstacles most commonly stood in the way of achieving their goals. Their answers fell broadly into three groups; chronic health problems; parenthood; and adjusting to change.

Let's look at these, and some other common obstacles, in closer detail.

Chronic Health Problems

As someone who has suffered with chronic mental health problems all of my life, I absolutely understand this problem. Whether it's chronic pain, depression, an autoimmune disorder, or something else, having a long-term condition that affects your day-to-day life can be a huge challenge when it comes to achieving your goals. These health problems can be unpredictable and difficult to plan for. When I'm laying out my publishing schedule for the year, I can't possibly predict that I'll spend all of April in the foetal position, unable to get dressed because the world is freaking me out.

It may be the case that over the years you've learned ways to minimise the effects of your condition. Perhaps certain dietary choices, or regular fresh air help; maybe it's regular acupuncture, or the right balance of socialising; or it might be the right medication that's essential. If you have sure-fire methods of regulating your health, make sure these are included in your plan for your time. Don't neglect your health needs in favour of cramming in an extra 1000 words.

When an unexpected flare-up occurs, the most important thing you can do is be gentle with yourself. There is no benefit to getting frustrated or despondent, or blaming your condition. First and foremost, address your health needs – seek qualified help if necessary, get support from someone who understands what you're going through. Don't ignore the problem or try to "power through" it. Face it and get help. It's the only way to be able to move forward.

Parenthood and Working From Home

Everyone who works from home faces one general problem: distraction.

When home is your place of work, rest, and play, it can be extremely difficult to maintain boundaries around these areas of your life. Many of us, especially those of us with children, know the pain of trying to work when there are other things, or people, clawing for your attention absolutely all of the time. Even if you don't have children there is a very good chance that you sometimes feel the pull of Netflix, or the kitchen, or a quick walk outside, or any number of other distractions that can get in the way of a good day's writing.

When I'm focused on a first draft, particularly during NaNoWriMo when it is full pedal to the metal, I have to make arrangements to minimise these distractions. Things like having the kids go and stay with my parents for a few days, disconnecting my internet, and so on, but these solutions are not practical long-term. They can be sustained for short bursts, before other demands take over and that carefully cultivated distraction-free time disappears.

Much of how you handle these distractions will be unique to your personality and your situation, but I can help with some general tips for mitigating a variety of different distractions around the home.

Designate different spaces for work and other activities: This might be a home office, a desk in a corner of a room, or perhaps simply writing on a laptop on one sofa seat and sitting somewhere else to watch TV. Whatever small tweaks you can make to trick your brain into associating one place with work and another with other activities.

Work outside the home if possible: Many writers enjoy writing in a cafe, or library, or outside when the weather allows. You might even find it helpful to rent an office space or co-working space. I wrote the bulk of my first two books at the library. My children were very young and I would leave them at home with my mum while I went to the library for a couple of hours. It served the dual function of giving me some child-free time, and getting lots of words written. I encourage you to try finding ways to leave the home to write, as you may well find that there are fewer distractions when away from home. Even in a bustling cafe or coffee shop, the ambient noise may help you to focus, rather than causing a distraction. Just ensure that your Wi-Fi is turned off so that you don't end up turning to the internet as a means of procrastination. If you don't have family who can help with childcare, explore other options, such as reciprocal arrangements with another parent.

Timetable yourself: Go back to school and write out an actual timetable for yourself. Designate time to write, time to focus on marketing or admin, and, crucially, time to eat and to relax. Broadly speaking we seem to fall into one of two camps: either an inability to stop working and chill out, or an inability to get focused on work or writing. They are two sides of the same coin. It's because our brains can't separate out our lives into these chunks when everything is happening in the same venue. When there is no choice but to do everything at home at least some of the time, we need to use every tool available to get our brains to work in our favour. Scheduling out your time can be a really constructive way to do this, whether your weakness is for overwork or under-work. I know some writers forget to stop for lunch, or have trouble clocking off at the end of the day. I myself am guilty of trying to get things done on my phone, like writing podcast scripts, or replying to emails, when I'm supposed to be spending quality time with my kids.

It's easy to make excuses for ourselves, and a lot of self-employed people do this. It is by no means unique to writers. Smartphones have made it very easy to be constantly available. So dedicate set times for yourself when work is not an option and, likewise, when social media and email are not options because you need to focus on writing. Schedule dedicated windows of time to different items. Have a physical timetable in your planner, or on your wall if it helps. Above all, have periods of time that are clearly designated as time off. These should be chunks of each and every day, and also a whole day whenever you can spare one. Rope them off and factor that in when deciding how much time you have for work or writing each week, or month.

Airplane mode: Leading on from that last point, make good use of the flight mode on your phone. I switch mine to flight mode when I need to stop myself from being distracted by social media or games. I also flick it on at 10pm every night and don't switch it off until 9am.

That time is phone-free as it is primarily my sleep and relaxation time. On a similar note, and I go on about this one a lot, please turn off your notifications! Even when your phone is not in airplane mode, you don't want to be always at the mercy of the dings. There is virtually nothing that can't wait an hour. Allowing your phone to dictate what gets your attention is a colossal time suck, so please take steps to minimise its interference in your life.

Get help: I am a big believer in outsourcing wherever possible. We are not superheroes. We cannot possibly do all of the things that modern life seems to demand of us. So ask for help. If you have a partner, make sure you have the housework equally shared between you, and ensure they are doing their fair share of the parenting if you have children. If there is something extra that they can take off your plate, let them do that for you.

If you're in the financial position to do so, consider hiring a cleaner to take on some of the housework. Make use of other family or childcare to help free up some of your time. This will allow you to give your full attention to your children more often, rather than being forever torn in two. If money is a concern, don't despair, there are free options. I have a friend who had a continuous flow of Workaway guests in her home while she was a single parent. Workaway is a genius system where people from other countries get to come and stay with hosts for free in exchange for doing unpaid work. That might be help in a garden or on an allotment, help around the house, or whatever the host needs. My friend had house and childcare help from these wonderful, enthusiastic young people who were on their travels around the world. It worked perfectly for her.

You might also get to a stage in your career when you can hire a personal, or virtual assistant to help you with your admin. Or you might be able to outsource the management of your ads. Be sure this makes good financial sense for you first, but this can be a game changer when it comes to managing your time between work and home.

One thing is for certain: working from home is a minefield of potential pitfalls. We all have so many demands on our time and attention; carving out dedicated periods of work, rest, and play is essential if we are going to meet our goals while also retaining our sanity and maintaining our health.

 Exercise

Think about some of the things you can do to minimise distractions, delineate your areas of focus, and make the most of the advantages of working from home.

Adjusting to Change

Many of us are thrown for a loop when it comes to adjusting our plans when a big change occurs. We saw this first hand in March 2020 when we were all suddenly, unprecedentedly, placed under effective house arrest for an indefinite amount of time. Who could have seen that coming? Lives were completely upended, with parents of school children suddenly devoid of their usual child-free time, people out of work, businesses failing left right and centre, everyone unable to see extended family. All of that chaos placed a tremendous strain on everyone, and has disrupted the plans of virtually every writer.

Smaller changes can also interfere with our plans. And they don't have to be negative. Perhaps a new opportunity coming your way, a chance to collaborate with someone, or an event to go to. All of these are exciting things that could potentially move your author business forward. Adapting your plans to accommodate them is often a smart decision. But always check in with your big why to make sure that the new opportunity is aligned with what you are trying to achieve.

We talked at some length in Chapter 4 about keeping your plan for the year somewhat flexible, with room for adjustments. I would like to add that this is an important mindset. Being open to new ideas and resilient to unforeseen delays or challenges is a big part of any creative business. Sometimes you'll have frustrating technical problems come up, or a collaboration that goes awry, or a cover designer who lets you down. We all experience these setbacks, and being able to lift your chin and keep going is an important part of being in this business.

Always be sure that you give some thought to, without worrying about, the things that could possibly go wrong. It's good to be informed and aware, so that you can prepare yourself. Don't dig too deep into that pit and end up lost and buried in doubt and fear; it's a fine balance but one well worth striking.

As long as you leave enough room in your plan for some flexibility, you should be covered.

Other Obstacles

Imposter Syndrome

I don't know a single writer who has never felt a nagging voice inside saying, "Who do you think you are to write a book?" Sometimes that voice can stop us in our tracks and delay the completion or publication of a book. We give it far too much validity. We listen and we actually believe the traitor trying to rob us of our dreams and stop us achieving our goals. That nasty little voice somehow rings with authority.

Where does that voice come from? From every time

you were told to be more realistic, to scale back your ambitions, that there's no future in a creative career, that you should get a "real job". Whenever you hear or read about successful writers being rejected hundreds of times before finally getting a book accepted by a publisher, a seed of doubt is planted that this path is arduous and only for the elite. Gatekeepers in the publishing industry are there to keep ordinary people like you from embarrassing yourself by putting pages and pages of drivel out into the world.

These seeds get watered every time the story is encountered again, and again, and again. They flourish and become deeply rooted beliefs. You've come to know in your core that only the most special, the most gifted people are allowed to live a fulfilling and creative life. Only the most dedicated, the most skilled experts, have a right to be successful.

Here's the truth: that voice is a liar. It doesn't understand creativity, and it doesn't understand you. It's that bitter old man who did go get a "real job" and now lives a miserable existence devoid of any spark of intuition or sprinkle of magic. The voice belongs to someone who quit and who won't be satisfied until everyone else quits too.

It stalks you and strikes when you experience the tiniest wobble of doubt in your own abilities. There it is to tell you to give up.

The only thing you can do is hit mute. Block that little shit. You don't need that kind of toxic negativity in your life. You can decide not to listen to it ever again.

Look, I know it's not really that easy. That meanie is sat on my shoulder right now, tapping on my temple and telling me I've never really achieved anything. Asking me who I am to tell other people how to do it. So I'm writing this for myself, as well as you. He's a liar! Don't listen. Give him the brush-off and take a deep breath.

Here's a new inner voice for you: You ARE good enough, your voice matters. No one else in the world can write the book you're writing now, because no one else has your voice, your perspective, or your experience. You CAN write that book and you CAN publish it, if you choose to. You do not need anyone's permission to be creative, or to be successful.

The gatekeepers never really cared about quality. They only cared about sales. We are so fortunate to live in a time when we can choose *ourselves*, and kick open the gates. Independent publishing gives us the option to take full control of our writing careers, and carve our own paths. We can pour effort into creating wonderful stories to share with the world and then just share them — on our own terms.

Shove that imposter demon off your shoulder. You don't need to lug around the extra weight of all its emotional baggage.

Perfectionism

Imposter syndrome has a twin: a more attractive sibling who comes to you dressed in finery and acting like your friend. She slinks up to you, strokes your face, and tells you that you can make your book better if you just add this, and remove that, and tweak the other thing. She drapes herself over your shoulders and whispers these sweet nothings to you endlessly. Literally. She will never go away. No matter what you do to try to shake her off, she sticks around like an infection.

She is not your friend. She is not trying to help. She is just as insidious as the bitter old bastard that you just sent packing.

Now, don't get me wrong, there is nothing wrong with wanting to make your writing better, or wanting to put out a high quality book, but perfectionism not only gets in the way of finishing a project, it can stop you from even starting. That's the problem. That's the temptress you have to say goodbye to. She's a serious obstacle to you achieving your goals.

In the words of writer Rebecca Solnit, "So many of us believe in perfection, which ruins everything else, because the perfect is not only the enemy of the good; it's also the enemy of the realistic, the possible, and the fun."

Writing should be an opportunity to explore, play, rebel,

and above all, create. There's no room for the creativity-blocker of "perfect". Perfect is impossible. Nothing can ever be perfect. It's a fantasy, not a real goal to pursue. What does it even mean? It's subjective. One person's "perfect" is another person's "flawed". No matter how much energy and attention you pour into a project, someone somewhere is going to dislike it, or find fault with it. It's inevitable.

Make your writing the best it can reasonably be, and then release it. Let go of the idea that it has to be perfect, and get on with creating the next thing.

"Go and make interesting mistakes, make amazing mistakes, make glorious and fantastic mistakes. Break rules. Leave the world more interesting for your being here. Make. Good. Art."

— Neil Gaiman

Identify Your Obstacles

I like to give some thought each week to what might stand in the way of me achieving my goals. I know what my weaknesses are, and because I do a weekly review to see what worked and what didn't, I usually go into the new week with some ideas of things that could be pitfalls. For example, if I know that I'm starting the week not feeling well, I know that my health could prevent me from accomplishing as much as I usually do. So I adjust my expectations accordingly. Or perhaps I know in advance that my usual childcare won't be available, then I know I will have fewer hours available to work and, again, adjust my expectations.

Productivity and accomplishment are a constant flow of adjusted expectations. This is why flexibility is so important when setting your goals. SMART goals should never be completely rigid. They are specific and time-bound and all of that good stuff, but remember that the A stands for "attainable" after all. Build in the required flexibility to that aspect of the goal, as well as giving yourself enough time in the deadline that you set.

Ultimately, knowledge is power. If you have taken some time at each stage of your goal-setting to identify potential problems, you can better prepare for them.

This is particularly effective on the weekly level, as described above, but it should be a factor when scheduling your year as well. For instance, I never plan to do lots of work in December, because a rather obvious obstacle to me accomplishing a lot of work that month is a huge increase in the amount of time that I intend to spend with my family. I know, for example, that it would be foolish to plan a book launch for the 18th of December

Obstacles aren't necessarily "bad" things that we want to avoid. They are simply things that might prevent progress towards a specific goal. They might be things that advance a different goal.

Some we can plan for in advance, like my December example, but some crop up unexpectedly. That's why we check in regularly and make note of them. In our accountability group, Unstoppable Authors, each week I lay out what I want to achieve, I note potential obstacles and, crucially, I think of ways to mitigate those obstacles. If my kids are going through a phase of staying up late, common in the summer with the lighter evenings, I know that one obstacle might be less time in the evenings for podcast recording. So I think about ways around this. That might include keeping my other half informed of my schedule so that he can take on the evening parenting solo while I work. Or it might be that recording needs to happen at another time. I encourage the other authors in the group to do this too.

The final step of planning a way around those obstacles is vital. It's no good identifying problems and then doing nothing about them. Always factor this in to your regular check-ins.

Crisis and Survival Modes

One final word about this. I won't go on about it too much as I did cover it at the start of the book. But I feel that it is worth mentioning again here while we are on the subject of handling obstacles as these will be the biggest obstacles of all.

So many of us come to a grinding a halt when life throws us illness, emergency, or loss. And I want to state here for the record that it is okay to stop.

Please, please, if you only take one thing from this book, let it be that you are allowed to stop writing, stop planning, stop everything, when a disaster happens and you are forced into crisis mode.

Your writing and your goals will still be there for you when it passes. That is the thing about crises, they all pass. They are, by definition, temporary.

Survival mode, however, is a different beast. This is a mode that can stick around for a long time. Your survival mode might be living with a chronic condition, or having separated from a partner and experiencing a long period of adjustment. Perhaps it's having a relative for whom you need to become a full time carer.

When you're in survival mode, you never have enough time for stretching yourself, growing a business, increasing your word output, or learning new skills. In survival mode, you have to be okay with getting by on the bare minimum.

Tips for Surviving Survival Mode

'Enough' Lists

I recommend taking some time to pause and look at your life objectively. Break down your life into different areas, such as parenting, writing, relationships, and so on. Don't get too granular or this will take far longer than necessary. For each area of your life that you've identified, write down a few things that you could do and still feel that you were doing just enough. This is your bare minimum. Under parenting, for example, it might include "read to my children each day" or "connect with them each day". Under relationships, you might include "take a walk together each week". Whatever it is for you personally that is enough for you to feel that you have done your part to nurture that area of your life.

These 'enough' lists will be your guide during times of survival mode. Study them regularly and never give yourself a hard time for failing to do more than the minimum. On my 'enough' list for my writing life, I just have two items:

It is enough that I continue to write and publish.

It is enough that I am part of the author community.

That's all. There is no suggestion of how often I need to publish, or how many words I need to write. There is no onus on me to do all of the things. Just those two simple things that can be done at my own, flexible pace.

Be gentle with yourself. Be realistic in your expectations, especially if you have a health problem yourself or are a carer for someone else. Health always comes first. Look after yourself and be content to *just do enough*.

ACE

One of my favourite tricks I've been using for a couple of years now is to ACE every single day, and I have never missed one since I started. It's very simple, provided you already use some sort of planner.

At the end of each day when I sit down with my bullet journal, I note down one thing that I **accomplished**, one way I **connected** with someone, and one thing I **enjoyed**. No matter what darkness is clouding my life, I can always think of something for each of these categories. Even if my only accomplishment is getting dressed even though I didn't want to, or that my only connection was cuddling my cat for ten minutes; these little things count and can always help me to end each day feeling as though I did enough.

Accomplished

Connected

Enjoyed

During periods of productivity and good mental health, I might have several things to choose from for one or more of the ACEs. That's great! But I still only include one as a general rule. I use longer form journaling to chronicle in more detail my other noteworthy achievements. For the accomplishment in particular, I try not to include something that is marked as complete from my task list. I try to find something additional to include. For instance, preparing a healthy meal, working out, or calling a friend might make the list. If I hit a milestone, like finishing a first draft, setting a launch date, or getting a new personal best in the gym, it gets celebrated here. I even give myself gold stars!

The ACE technique has helped me get through some lengthy periods of survival mode. I highly recommend you give it a try.

Shorter-Term Planning

I've walked you through my system, which includes setting annual, quarterly, and monthly goals. I find this system to be an ideal blend of structure and flexibility. However, there may be situations in life where longer-term planning simply isn't valuable or possible. At times, we don't quite know what is going to happen in a few weeks, never mind a few months.

In times like these, or when you're in survival mode, a shorter timeframe for your plans might be the perfect thing you need in order to still get things done. This can easily be done by adapting the quarterly framework into a six-week period. Where I described setting up a list of goals and action steps for a three-month period and breaking it down into three, month-long chunks, you can condense that into a six-week block, and divide it into two-week chunks.

My advice for doing this is to pick one goal to focus on at a time. Six weeks will often fly by, and the point of using this structure is to cope with an unpredictable situation and be able to adapt. So don't try to pile as much into six weeks as you would plan to do in three months.

Get focused. Pick one project that you can realistically complete, or make significant progress on, in a six-week period. That probably won't be "write a book", but it might, if you're a rapid writer. If it's coming up to a cycle of NaNoWriMo, then it could be the perfect goal. Perhaps a week to prepare, 30 days to write the words, and a week to tidy those words up.

Your goal for a short blast of focused time might be to launch a book. Two weeks to recruit a street team and pitch podcasters, bloggers, and so on. Two weeks to create a tonne of content. And finally two weeks of promoting your new book around the launch date.

Maybe six weeks is the perfect amount of time to break a habit, or form a new one. Or perhaps it's the perfect opportunity to declutter your home.

There are an infinite number of things you could fit into six weeks, and when the time is up you can move on to the next right thing in another six-week block. So if life demands this sort of adjustment to your planning, then go ahead and use it.

The key thing I really want to emphasise in all of this is that what matters is that your system must work for you. Find a rhythm, a timescale, and a system that fits with your unique life and goals.

When you're in survival mode, find ways to keep creating, keep achieving. Lower your expectations, be realistic, of course, but don't stop. Find ways to carve creativity into your life. One day, survival mode will pass, and you'll be glad you kept on creating.

"WRITE IT. SHOOT IT. PUBLISH IT. CROCHET IT, SAUTÉ IT, WHATEVER — MAKE."

—Joss Whedon

Chapter 9: Embrace Your Spark of Madness

"YOU'RE ONLY GIVEN A LITTLE SPARK OF MADNESS, YOU MUSTN'T LOSE IT."

— Robin Williams

Don't forget the fun

We've just been talking about some fairly heavy stuff. The challenges and difficulties of life. I've asked you to do some pretty intensive planning, some of it quite long-term. So I wanted to circle back around to why you got into this writing gig in the first place. Chances are, it's to do with happiness. You want to write because you love telling stories, or because you want to move people, or because you have an innate creative spark that demands the chance to burn as a full flame.

Please don't ever lose sight of that.

Did you make your big why something to do with this passion for words? Frame it, keep it nearby.

All of this detailed goal setting should always come back to the fun stuff; the joy, the thrill of crafting the perfect plot twist or redemption. When you structure your days and weeks in such a way as to maximise your chances of achieving those lofty sales goals, or publication deadlines, always make sure there is room for fun! For the sheer exhilaration of crafting your stories.

As writers, we may have a bit of a reputation for being dark, gloomy, solitary figures. The tortured artist, if you will. But you and I both know that that stereotype is very often wrong. Not many of us are actually like that. At least not past our early twenties, when we stop wearing all black and moping about thinking that the entire world revolves around us.

We know really, whatever stage of our writing journey we happen to be at, that it is a tremendous honour and privilege to be a conduit for these magnificent ideas, one that enriches our lives far more than it drains them. Because there's no denying that the act of creating that novel can be like wrestling an alligator. It can be frustrating, laborious, and infuriating when it doesn't go smoothly, but we wouldn't change a thing when we get to know the satisfaction of typing "The End", or better yet, of holding our book in our hands for the first time. Every drawn out word, every hour spent staring at the blank screen, every night of lost sleep because the characters wouldn't stop nattering in our heads; the blood, sweat, and tears is all worth it in the end.

When it isn't a struggle, when we experience "flow" and the words come with ease, it can be like riding the most epic roller coaster. It's an amazing feeling to pour words out onto the page, to see our stories taking shape. When we manage to transpose a vague idea into something of substance that has the potential to take readers on a tremendous journey along with our complex characters, *that* is when we know that what we do is important. We do the seemingly impossible. We give life to ideas.

This is no less significant than the brilliant minds that brought us the light bulb, or the rocket, or hell, even the wheel. It's all part of the same system – the transference of intangible idea into substantial application. We may not physically move people around the globe, or into space, with the fruition of our ideas, but we can take people anywhere in their imaginations. We can influence opinion, we can change societies. Our words may one day be studied by young and impressionable minds as an example of exemplary human endeavour. And even if that is never likely to be the case, we can still move people with words. Just words.

The value of that is not to be underestimated.

I do hope that this concept hasn't alarmed you. I'm sure a great many writers out there have no lofty ambitions to become the subject of study in literature classes. I don't wish to force upon you any enormous sense of obligation or responsibility. I just wish to encourage you to value your writing. It matters, if only to you. Even if you never publish a word, if it has brought you joy, or a thrill, then it matters.

Most of all, I want you to put down this book feeling that you are ready to experience all of the wonderful emotions that come with the act of creating worlds and people and stories with your words. I want you, in the midst of the planning and aspiring, to remember the core of what it means to be a writer.

Make space in your life for these experiences and your life will be all the richer for it. I truly hope that the systems and tips I've shared in this book result in you accomplishing more of your goals. But far more importantly, I hope that these systems help you to balance your life in such a way that you have time to appreciate the fun!

Conclusion: The Hero Returns

"WHEN YOU TAKE RISKS YOU LEARN THAT THERE WILL BE TIMES WHEN YOU SUCCEED AND THERE WILL BE TIMES WHEN YOU FAIL AND BOTH ARE EQUALLY IMPORTANT."

—Ellen DeGeneres

We've come to the end of our journey together, but it is far from the end of your journey as a writer. I hope that you now have a destination in mind, a map, and a plan for how to get there. I hope that you will use the SMART goal setting system and find accountability partners to help you reach your goals.

We are each on a unique path, crafting our own life story. My journey will look very different to yours, but we can always support one another and cheer each other along. Please know that I am cheering you on from my own lane. You don't need to jump into my lane and I don't need to join yours for us to support one another.

The framework that I've given you, along with the tips and tricks for actually accomplishing your goals, is one that you can return to again and again. You can adapt it for your own situation, too. Whatever struggles and obstacles you may encounter on the journey towards your goals, you now have the tools to help you cope with and adapt to the ones that stick around, and to overcome the less stubborn ones.

The final section of this book will list important resources for you going forward, and I do hope that you'll make use of them.

My final words to you are on the subject of failing. Please know that the systems in this book are only a guide, and there are absolutely no guarantees in life. We ALL fail sometimes. It's an essential part of the process of learning and growing. I've been a goal setting nerd for as long as I can remember, but I'm not some super-achieving wiz who never has a bad day, month, or year. Being okay with failing is an important part of this experience. Please don't shy away from risk for fear of failing.

Set your goals as high as you want, and strive for them with all of your might. You won't meet them all, you just won't, and that's fine. That's great! Because you can learn from those cases and adapt.

Above all, I hope that this book gives you the confidence to always be able to adapt to whatever life throws at you. I hope we never have another year like 2020, I truly do. But if there comes another absolute nightmare of a year for you or your wider community, these processes should help you to come through that time with some sense of accomplishment.

Resources

References

Gail Matthews' study on writing down goals:
www.dominican.edu/sites/default/files/2020-02/gailmatthews-harvard-goals-researchsummary.pdf

Yoga lowers cortisol:
www.ncbi.nlm.nih.gov/pmc/articles/PMC3768222

Nature's impact on mental health:
www.sciencedaily.com/releases/2019/04/190404074915.htm
www.health.harvard.edu/mind-and-mood/sour-mood-getting-you-down-get-back-to-nature

Productivity Resources

Bullet Journal:
Ryder Carroll's website:
bulletjournal.com/pages/about
Buy his book, The Bullet Journal Method
books2read.com/u/bQKjEw

Trello:
trello.com

Amazon book description formatting:
kindlepreneur.com/amazon-book-description-generator

Workaway:
www.workaway.info

Author Resources

NaNoWriMo:
nanowrimo.org

Mailerlite:
www.mailerlite.com/invite/3f9a11ef1d585

Newsletter Ninja by Tammi L. Labreque:
books2read.com/u/3Lg0L0

Book Funnel:
bookfunnel.com

Scrivener:
www.literatureandlatte.com/scrivener/overview

Unstoppable Authors Podcast:
www.unstoppableauthors.com

Accountability

Unstoppable Authors group:
www.facebook.com/groups/weareunstoppableauthors

Get Your Free Planning Guide

If you subscribe to my Tribe, I will send you a collection of annual, quarterly, and monthly planning worksheets. You can use these on their own, or integrate them into a planner. Just let me know where to send your copy here:

www.subscribepage.com/goalsettingforwriters

Please Leave a Review

I hope you enjoyed Goal Setting for Writers. I would really appreciate it if you could take a few minutes now to review the book on your favourite retailer. Independent authors rely heavily on reader reviews, they really are like oxygen. Reviews help other readers decide whether a book is a good fit for them or not. Much as I want everyone to love my books, I also know that it's important to find the right readers, so just a few words from you could help me to do that and reach other readers who will benefit from the wisdom in this book.

Thank you!

Acknowledgements

This book would not have been possible without the unwavering support of my husband, Andy, and my patient children who are growing up with the phrase "Mummy has a deadline".

I'd also like to thank my editor, Zoë Markham, who never fails to fit me in to her schedule and is always pushing me to improve.

A big shout out to my amazing author friends who keep me accountable and motivated, who listen when I need to talk through a problem and who are always forthcoming with possible solutions. Particular thanks to Angeline, Julia, Sacha, Dan, and Meg for providing feedback on this book.

Finally, thank you to my Patrons; Andy, Emé, Linzy, Richard, Martin, and Monika. You've stuck by me during a challenging time and I appreciate you all so much.

About the Author

Holly Lyne lives in Yorkshire, UK, with her husband, two children and cat. When not juggling family commitments, she writes dark urban fantasy novels, purging her imagination of its demons. Inspired by the King of Horror himself, Holly aspires to be at least half as prolific and successful and promises to limit herself to only one tome of The Stand-like proportions in her career. Holly is a proud geek and bullet journal enthusiast with a knack for being organised and getting shit done.

Check out my website for all the latest updates and offers - hblyne.com

Follow me on:

> Instagram - instagram.com/hblyne/
>
> Facebook - facebook.com/authorhblyne
>
> YouTube - youtube.com/channel/ UCaSXi1qHF3nv2axlV6MYnCA
>
> Patreon - patreon.com/hblyne

Fiction by H.B. Lyne

The Shifters of Caerton series:

Fate of the Blue Moon

Ghosts of Winter

Demons of the Past

Rise of the Furies

Dark Echoes: Tales from the Shadows

From Ashes to Echoes

Lies the Dead Tell series:

In The Blood

Printed in Great Britain
by Amazon